Living
Your
Dreams

Also by Mark Victor Hansen

BOOKS

Chicken Soup for the Soul series—254 different books in print

The Aladdin Factor

ASK!

Cash in a Flash

Cracking the Millionaire Code

Dare to Win

Dreams Don't Have Deadlines

How to Make the Rest of Your Life the Best of Your Life

Master Motivator

The Miracle of Tithing

The Miracles in You

The One Minute Millionaire

Out of the Blue

The Power of Focus

The Richest Kids in America

Speed Edit Your First Book

Speed Write Your Amazing Publishing Plan

Speed Write (and Deliver) Your Killer Speech

Speed Write Your First Book

Speed Write Your First Screenplay

Speed Write Your Mega Book Marketing Plan

Speed Write Your Personal Life Story

U R the Solution

Visualizing Is Realizing

You Have a Book in You

AUDIOS

How to Think Bigger than You Ever Thought You Could Think

Dreams Don't Have Deadlines

Visualizing Is Realizing

Sell Yourself Rich

Chicken Soup for the Soul series

The One Minute Millionaire

Cracking the Millionaire Code

LIVING YOUR DREAMS

Your Personal Success Program

Mark Victor Hansen

Published 2020 by Gildan Media LLC
aka G&D Media
www.GandDmedia.com

Front Cover design by David Rheinhardt of Pyrographx

Interior design by Meghan Day Healey of Story Horse, LLC

Library of Congress Cataloging-in-Publication Data is available upon request

ISBN: 978-1-7225-0311-6

10   9   8   7   6   5   4   3   2   1

CONTENTS

PREFACE To Live Your Dreams 7

INTRODUCTION 13

ONE What You Want Wants You 35

TWO Believe It and Achieve It 53

THREE Positive Self-Talk 71

FOUR Turning Problems into Assets 87

FIVE The Fundamental Secrets of Prosperity 109

SIX Gain Financial Freedom 141

SEVEN Create a Dream Team 169

EIGHT Achieving Total Well-Being 191

NINE Awaken Your Spirit 207

TEN Ten Instant Steps to Success 223

To Live Your Dreams

The possibilities you imagine for yourself are some-times so audacious that you don't want to tell any-one for fear they will laugh, criticize, and castigate you. Don't deny your dreams; instead let each of them excite you in the fiber of your being.

You have extraordinary possibilities. You want so very much, and it's all wonderful. You have big, bold, and daring dreams. There are infinite possibilities, ideas, hunches, inklings, and inner nudges waiting inside you. They are called *dreams*.

You have God-sized dreams—so dynamic that you are almost intimated by them. Dreams to be, do, and have more. Dreams of creating wealth, health, happiness, and outstanding relationships. Dreams of falling forever in love with your ideal mate. Dreams of having cherished children and grandchildren. Dreams of health and happiness for your family. Dreams of financial, political, social, and geographic freedom. Dreams for the company or companies you want to create. Dreams of innovations and inventions that will improve and transform the world. Dreams of positively affecting a billion people in the next decade. Dreams of creating great and inspiring books, plays, and movies. Dreams of having a life-enriching education that enables you to master the principles of achievement. Dreams of being a visionary leader, acting courageously, purposefully, and with impact. Dreams of gaining respect, renown, fame, and fortune. Dreams of finding new worlds here and in the heavens above. Dreams of traveling to distant lands, meeting wonderful people, and having friends around the world. Dreams of being a powerful creator of your best and most rewarding experiences. Dreams of having an expansive, exhilarating, and superb life.

This book is about bringing those dreams into reality and living them every day. When you cogitate, ruminate, and meditate on your dreams, they ultimately and inevitably become your reality.

Let me share some examples that I hope will inspire you to dream bigger and better and live more of your dreams as you launch into this life-transforming book.

At age fifteen, my late, great friend John Goddard set a life list of goals of becoming a world-renowned adventurer, explorer, author, lecturer, and friend to the leaders of the world. He wrote a list of 127 audacious, exciting, and incredible experiences and achievements, practically all of which he accomplished.

John and I hiked together regularly and rigorously. We spent days together thinking out loud about what's possible. We pushed each other's vocabularies to the limit, inspiring each other's thinking and mind expansion.

I took many friends through John's artifact-rich home museum, and each one was astounded at his depth of wisdom, knowledge, experience, and love for humanity and our planet.

I had John speak at many of my seminars around the country. At one class in Sedona, Arizona, we asked our students to rise before dawn. John took us to where few humans have ever been allowed. With tribal permission, we hiked and explored through ancient, sacred Zuni Indian ruins. While touring the ruins, John, an archaeologist and anthropologist, showed us the hieroglyphs and petroglyphs and discussed them with illuminating insights. I hope his visions will inspire you at the depth of your soul to write new dreams of your own into your future.

The second classic story of dreamers comes from the brothers Orville and Wilbur Wright, who were mechanics with an impossible dream. Owners of a bicycle shop, they dreamed that humans would be able to fly. Their father, a man of the cloth, said, "Boys, if man was meant to fly, he'd be born with wings." In 1903, at Kitty Hawk, North Carolina, they flew only twelve seconds, traveled 120 feet, and reached a top speed of 6.8 miles per hour, but their dream created the trillion-dollar aviation industry.

Allow me to share the story of one more man who is living his dreams. Elon Musk, born in South Africa, came to Stanford University in California, where he became friends with Peter Thiel. They created PayPal, and each became billionaires. Elon wrote down five giant dreams when he was at the university in 1995. He wanted to be involved in:

- Sustainable energy (production and consumption)
- The Internet
- Space exploration
- Artificial intelligence
- Rewriting human genetics

I believe that Elon is the greatest and most courageous thinker, inventor, innovator, visionary leader, and doer of our time. He has succeeded brilliantly with PayPal, SpaceX, Tesla, Neuralink, and Solar City. He has giant dreams of changing the electric battery by making it affordably last over a million hours. He is competing now with Jeff Bezos and Richard Branson to have the first company rocket ship that goes to Mars, colonizes it, and returns safely with the astronauts.

As this writing, Elon has become the fourth richest man in the world. When the coronavirus shut down most auto manufacturers, Tesla included, he wouldn't have it. Elon saw that ventilators were desperately needed, so he called the 3M company, who could not manufacture them fast enough. Elon said: "I have metal, 3D printers, and skilled craftsmen, and I will joint-venture with your company." He did and was supersuccessful in delivering on his promised ventilators, but simultaneously he kept making ninety thousand Teslas. They sold briskly into a market that was hungry for superior electric vehicles. They are not just cars; they are computers on wheels, equipped with batteries with silicon chips. These self-driving vehicles use AI to repair themselves and have made Tesla the world leader in electric vehicles.

It costs nothing to dream big, so dream bigger than big. Know that the rewards, recognition, and excitement will be both enormous and fun. When we meet (which I predict we will), I want to hear how you are living your dream.

Otherwise please consider sharing your story with me at: reception@markvictorhansen.com.

Remember, you have your dreams, and then your dreams have you.

Mark Victor Hansen
Scottsdale, Arizona
October 2020

INTRODUCTION

Congratulations! You are now taking action that separates you from those who merely dream about a life worth living. You have taken the first step to being one of those rare people who have decided in favor of themselves. You're deciding to live your dreams. It's a life transforming step that will exalt your life forever.

Everyone has hopes of achieving an extraordinary quality of life. You've distinguished yourself from the masses with a commitment to make your dreams a reality. You wouldn't be reading this book right now unless you had made a conscious decision to take charge of your own destiny. With that decision made, now is the time to stretch yourself and open your mind with new concepts and ideas that will propel you to live your dreams.

Your mind is your most powerful tool. The ideas in this book can be your ticket to anywhere. In fact, life itself is a ticket that will take you wherever you want to go. The question is, where do you want to go?

That's what we'll explore together in this book in hopes of motivating, inspiring, and empowering you to make a significant, meaningful, and fulfilling life for yourself so that you can to live your dreams.

After all, when your life is over, you will have traded it for something. The *something* you get—what you will have given your whole life for—can only be made meaningful and important by you. All meaning is self-induced.

In your dreams, we all aspire to be, do, and have great things, yet most of us simply aren't creating the results we want. We don't have enough money, romance, success, or joy in our lives. We need to understand that greatness exists in all of us, and it is up to us to pull it out of ourselves, individually and collectively.

It's been said that we all have genius; we just need to learn to apply it. As you read, absorb, and think through this book, write out three superpowers that you know you have that could exalt you to genius status. We all have them, but unfortunately, in most people they lie dormant, never to be explored, investigated, or realized. This book is here to help you discover your superpowers and supercharge you onward, upward, and Godward.

The average person could probably list three good reasons to prove why they can't achieve whatever it is they want, but deep down in our hearts don't we know that we could do it all if we only dared to live our dreams? Is it possible that the only thing holding us back is fear?

Of course. It's fear that thwarts us, stalemates us, stifles us, erodes our self-esteem, and places imaginary roadblocks in our path. Fear keeps us from taking action, and if we don't act, we will never get beyond where we are now.

But our fears disappear when we confront them. Once we take charge of ourselves, we can be, do, and have anything and everything we ever dreamed of second by second. We are either mobilized to take action or immobilized and stuck in a quagmire of complacency.

I don't know what's keeping you from what you really want, but from my decades of coaching millions of people around the world, I know that everything the mind can conceive and believe, it can achieve, so let's start right now, today, to live your dreams.

If you're alive, you have a destiny to fulfill. You have to command your inner self to magnify, multiply, and magnetize your talents and abilities to their fullest expression. A happy, wealthy, fulfilled, and prosperous life is yours for the asking. You might want more money or perhaps a more stimulating job or career. Maybe you want true love or a more gratifying sexual relationship. You might secretly dream of being in the movies, being president of your own corporation, entering politics, saving the environment, or becoming a world-transforming philanthropist.

We all aspire to bigger and better things, yet many of us simply aren't getting the results we want. We don't have enough money, romance, success, or joy in our lives. We don't feel fulfilled or satisfied. Why? Because of excuses.

Why aren't we all that we want to be? Why don't we have all that we want? Why aren't we prosperous and blessed with the world's abundance? What's keeping us from having it all? If I ask the average person, I'm sure they could give me plenty of good reasons for not succeeding—"I'm too ugly, too fat, too skinny. I'm too young, I'm too old. I'm too tall, I'm too short. I'm not smart enough. I'm too weak or too strong. I'm from a minority group or a majority group. I don't have the education, or I have too much education. I'm overqualified or unqualified. I'm just a woman or just a man. I'm too bald, or I'm too hairy. I'm a single parent, or I've been married five times. I'm just a wife or a husband.

I'm a loser two or three times over, and it's even tat-
tooed on my arm."

Are these truly good reasons? Are these excuses
holding us back? Or is it rather that we don't want to
fulfill our dreams badly enough? Or is it that we think
we don't deserve it?

Excuses are always there, but desire is inside. It's
in our chest, gripping our hearts, and telling us we are
afraid.

In our culture, we don't like admitting that we're
afraid of anything other than direct physical violence.
"How could I be afraid?" we say to ourselves. Yet we
all have fears. For some of us, it's fear of failure. If we
try and don't succeed, we might embarrass ourselves,
or we might even embarrass other people. For others,
it's a fear of success. Succeeding might be more fearful
than failing. If we succeeded in becoming president of
a corporation, we'd have to speak before large groups,
manage people, produce annual reports, be responsible
to stockholders, and be profitable. Possibly we'd have to
change some of our associates. Could we handle it? Do
we fear that we can't?

Danny DeVito, who is less than five feet tall,
became a massively successful television and movie
star, writer, and director. He overcame his fears rather
than letting his fears overcome him. We all need to
conquer our fears a little at a time. If we became movie

stars, could we handle the press, the critics, the work, the cameras? If we became prosperous, would we lose friendships, associates, the love of our family? What if we made more money than our parents or those we look up to? Would we be breaking some unwritten law or uncovering some hidden agenda or agendas? If success came all at once, would we know how to handle it? Would we know whom to trust?

Could hidden fears like these be the real roadblock rather than the excuses that we so easily mouth? I say the answer is yes. Most of us simply don't take the action necessary to be, do, or have what we really want.

Of course, almost no one would admit that to themselves, let alone somebody else. To protect our sensibilities and our subconscious disguises, our fears are perfectly reasonable, and our excuses sound good.

We may be bald or short or wear thick glasses, so we tell ourselves that we'll never find a perfect mate or be happily married. You may be just a woman or just a wife, or you might be fat or tall, so your hidden mind reasons that you could never attain an executive position in a male-dominated corporation and rise to the top. You've gone bankrupt and lost all your money and possessions, so you tell yourself you can't start a major corporation, invest in real estate, or tell others how to motivate their lives, right?

Wrong. You're listening to negative propaganda. You can't because you've convinced yourself you can't. Fear limits us, thwarts us, and stalemates us. The word *fear* may also be seen as an acronym: *False Evidence Appearing Real.* Fear creates stumbling blocks and leads to self-defeating behavior, which produces guilt and anxiety, which in turn lead to complete immobilization. Guilt always brings self-persecution. Fear keeps us from trying. If we don't try, we never get beyond where we are now, which in a convoluted way proves to us that we couldn't do it begin with.

After one of my seminars, a woman came up to me and complained that she couldn't go back to school because it would take five years to get a degree, and she'd be forty-three years old when she graduated. I couldn't help asking her, "How old will you be in five years if you *don't* go back to school and get a degree?"

The enemy is fear, be they big fears or a bunch of itty-bitty fears. Fear erodes our self-esteem, corrupts our self-confidence, and over time convinces us that we're losers. As long as we let fears control us, we'll never live our dreams.

We can learn to control our fears rather than let them control us. Fear can be defeated as long as we realize the source is inside us and not out there in the world. President Franklin Delano Roosevelt world is your oyster. Your life is a pearl of great price. It is too important to waste or squander. Commit to making it a masterpiece of a life well lived.

Ask yourself, "What do I really want, and what do I want five years from now?"

The trouble is, most of us have never been very clear about our desires. Most people don't know what they want but are pretty sure they haven't got it.

We know that the human mind has two basic parts—the conscious and the subconscious. We often fail to realize that while the conscious mind makes all the decisions, the subconscious mind makes all the provisions. Remember, you can't provide what you don't request and put in writing. The conscious mind determines what you want. The subconscious always figures out how to get it.

To put it another way, we all get in life what we expect to get. If we expect a lot, we get a lot. If we expect a little, we get a little. Great thinking attracts great results. Mediocre thinking attracts no results. Not thinking attracts nothing. Choose to become a positive, decisive, result-generating thinker who takes self-initiated action.

Each and every one of us has incredible resources in our mind. Our school system teaches us how to use our brains. That is, it teaches how to inventory and compute things, but it barely touches on the mind. The mind can think and go anywhere at once. The mind can figure out where you are and take you where you want to be. The world will stand aside and let any man or woman pass who knows where they want to go. You get whatever you expect. The only questions are, what do you really want? What do you really believe you have to do to get what you want? If you do what you have to do, then you'll get what you want to get.

Most people define their lives by what they *don't* want rather than by what they do want. One more time, let me ask, what do you want? Because if you ask for nothing, and get nothing, don't be surprised. When we use our minds creatively and constructively, it doesn't matter what we haven't done, haven't said, or haven't thought, but where we are now and where we want to go. We are forever starting over.

Start now to make yourself all you can be. The only thing that matters is how we engage the mind by telling our subconscious what we want to be. The philosopher Alfred North Whitehead said, "Great dreamers' dreams are never fulfilled. They're always transcended." In the same vein, Microsoft's Bill Gates said, "In the short term we expect too much; in the long term we don't expect enough."

In the 1980s, everyone thought that Chrysler was going to go bankrupt, but CEO Lee Iacocca said, "Chrysler will become the biggest and the best." While at Chrysler, he created the minivan. Iacocca dreamed a big and inspiring dream into realization and captured 75 percent of the minivan market at the time. He is now considered an American hero.

A lot of people have manifested their goals in areas ranging from fast food to smartphones. We can have anything we want if we direct our conscious mind and allow our subconscious to get it for us.

Next I want to talk to you about focused mind power. Success is creating a state of mind that creates results. Your belief determines your action. Your action determines your results. The feedback you get from good results generally improves your attitude and your future results, but first you have to believe that you can achieve. Choose to become a true believer in your own infinite possibilities.

Dr. Viktor Frankl, the author of *Man's Search for Meaning*, was one of the few survivors of Auschwitz. He was a German Jewish psychiatrist who somehow managed to live where tens of thousands of others died. With little food or clothing and no medical attention, he was forced to stand by while his fellow prisoners were cremated. Upon being released at the war's end, he was asked how he managed to survive, what powers he had that the others lacked.

Frankl's reply was very simple: "I always knew that my attitude was my own choice. I could choose to despair or be hopeful, but to be hopeful, I needed to focus on something I really wanted. I focused on holding my wife's hand one more time. I'm looking in her eyes deeply and penetratingly one more time. I'm hugging her and getting heart to heart, soul to soul one more time. That's all that I thought about, and it kept me alive second by second."

Frankl did not have more energy available to him than anyone else. He was frequently without food; on many days, all his captors gave him was one pea in a bowl of soup. Rather than squandering his energy in despairing about what was happening to him and those around him, he focused on that single goal—getting heart to heart, soul to soul, with his wife again, holding her hand, kissing her, resuming his love. That reason was so big and compelling and concentrated his energy so much that he was able to survive. Sure enough, the day came when he got back to her. He overcame, he persevered, and he became a powerful example of focusing your energy.

Focusing our energies in a single direction can work for us just as it worked for Frankl. If you're focused enough, you become like a laser beam, and you can really achieve breakthrough energy.

This truth was brought home to me at a relatively early age by my father. He came to the United States from Denmark in 1921. When he was seventeen years old, with an eighth-grade education, he was trained as a culinary artist to decorate giant cakes and other specially ordered baked goods. My father was immediately impressed by the United States as a land of opportunity. Unlike other countries, here you could do something, be something, have something, and work hard and get it. America offered political and economic freedom.

My father worked hard. While we were never rich, we were never poor. Father always said, "Free enterprise means the more enterprising you are, the freer you are." When I was nine years old, just old enough to ride a bike pretty well, I got a job delivering newspapers and carrying them in a sack from house to house. From my newspaper route, I earned enough money to buy a bicycle magazine, which I devoured it month after month. Long before European racing bicycles gained popularity here, I knew about them. They had low handlebars, thin tires, and narrow seats.

I saw the bike I wanted when my father took our family to live for a short time in Demark in 1957. I felt I could grow up and become a great cyclist. I was only missing one thing—a racing bike. I was determined to get that bike. I wanted it with my whole heart, mind, soul, and body. I had a picture of it hanging on the wall next to my bed; the caption said, "Ride a Wheel on Sheffield Steel."

From that picture, going into my dream state, I would visualize becoming a Windy City Wheeler in Chicago, riding four hundred miles a week and able to do fifty-mile marathon rides from Chicago to Milwaukee.

I could see it. I could feel it. I believed it. I had focused mind power, which is the strongest force in the universe. I didn't know what it was, but I knew it was going to work somehow. When I went to my dad and asked him for the bike again and again, he said, "Look, boy. I told you, you can have one when you're twenty-one."

"You don't understand, Dad," I said. "I don't want it when I'm twenty-one. I want it now. I'll be an old man when I'm twenty-one."

No kid wants deferred gratification. I kept badgering my father, and I finally hit him so hard that he conceded. He said, "I'll go down to sixteen, but don't ask again."

I knew that he was going to be pretty unbendable on this, so I hit him with his free enterprise rap: "Can I have the bike if I earned the money myself?" I'm sure my dad never dreamed that a nine-year-old could earn the then huge sum of $175. In 2020 dollars, that's about $1,619. My father had little to lose, so he agreed.

I wanted that racing bicycle so badly in my mind and my heart that I already owned it. All I had to do

point here is that everyone—introvert, extrovert, or omnivert—can learn to sell if they are selling something they believe in and that will benefit the customer. They will then earn the reward they truly want.

We're talking about focusing to produce outstanding results. I learned a lot from that experience. I learned the importance of working hard to get what you want, and I learned how to handle money. My father took half of my earnings and put it in my savings for college; he forced me to start my own savings account. When I matured and went to college, this forced savings was of great benefit to me. I still had three jobs to mostly pay my own way through college, but I thanked Dad in my prayers for his forced education. More importantly, he taught me a phenomenal work ethic, which he profoundly and quietly exemplified with excellence spirit and humility.

My father also taught me how to invest in stocks, although in a rather amateurish way. Most of all, I learned that when I really wanted something and focused all my energy on it, I could have it, because where the attention goes, the energy flows, and whatever you recognize, you energize. My mind power would show me the way and instruct me on how to do it so that I could have exactly what I wanted.

Once you know what you want, the resources of time, money, energy, and people show up. Once you are deeply committed, the universe conspires to fulfill your dreams, hopes, and desires. It's magical. It's mystical. It's like an acorn, which, once planted, watered, and fed, automatically attracts all that it needs to become a mighty oak. This was undoubtedly the most important lesson of all for me.

Next, I want to talk to you about abundance. If you don't have what you want, it could be that you haven't asked for it. Look around you. The world is filled with abundance. Nature is lavishly abundant. When I was upside down, uptight, and have-not, I visualized that someday I'd have my own home environment where we'd grow all of our own fresh fruits and vegetables. These days we grow organic produce well beyond what my family needs. We joyfully share the excess with staff, friends, and those in need. Today we have a kumquat tree in the backyard, and in one season we harvested over ten thousand kumquats from this little tree. We made kumquat jelly, kumquat jam, kumquat syrup.

We smilingly give kumquats to everybody on my staff.

If you really look with eyes of awareness, you see that there is fundamental abundance. The Hindu Upanishads, one of the oldest spiritual book on the planet, says in its first paragraph says: "Out of abundance, he or she took abundance and still abundance remains."

It's no longer how big a piece of the pie you get; it's how big you make the pie. The pie isn't out there; it's inside your own mind. Once you buy the idea that fundamental abundance is available to you inside, you'll start to discover it always and everywhere outside. It's not just for me, but for everybody.

In John 10:10, Jesus says, "I have come that you might have life and have it more abundantly." He was forever taking shortage and creating surplus and abundance. He also said: "Go and do likewise."

You probably know the parable of the loaves and the fishes. Jesus is out speaking to the masses. Over five thousand are in attendance. Back then, women and children were not counted, so there could have been twice or three times that many people. There were no fast-food places. Jesus asked his disciples to bring him food for everyone. They brought a little boy, who had five loaves and two fish. Jesus blessed this food, fed the masses completely, and had the disciples collect twelve baskets of leftovers. Jesus believed in, practiced, and taught from abundance without wasting anything. He also showed that there is always plenty if you have the right mindset and soul set.

In reality, this book is a time machine, and it can release you from the constraints of wanting. It can release you from have-notness and put you into fundamental haveness. Your thinking that there's enough will have you starting to manifest and see that there's more than enough for yourself and for everyone else.

I have discovered that while I earn a little fraction of a book price of, say, $10, many others benefit as well—the publisher, agents, editors, book designers, government trademark division, attorneys, accountants, printers, distributors, truckers, bookstores, their employees, my employees—who at the zenith amounted to 387 people.

The point is that $2 billion worth of my creations were sold at retail, along with $1 billion worth of licensed products, like T-shirts, greeting cards, minibooks, and even $157 million worth of Chicken Soup for the Soul Dog Food annually.

All of this started with one idea—to write a bestselling book and make it a series that becomes an empire. That is making the pie infinitely bigger.

So far I have written or cowritten 309 books and have many more in the pipeline (as well as other products and services.) I hope you are as excited to read about them as I am to write them. I see endless needs for information that I am both competent and eager to create. One of my giant dreams is to help half of our world population learn to read. As I point out in my book *ASK!*, reading in many ways is freedom. I share this with you because you can do the same or more.

I define an entrepreneur as someone who discovers a problem and fixes it for a vast profit. I am an entrepreneur who dreams of inspiring and teaching four billion non-readers to read. Yes, it's a mighty big goal, but what if I achieve it, or better yet, what if you figure out how to achieve it? Mother Teresa said: "I can do things that you cannot; you can do things that I cannot. Together we can do great things."

Know that I am cheering you on to the highest heights in order to make everyone better off and no one worse off. Abundance is available to you. Abundance awaits you. Abundance needs you, because only you can create it. Only you have your ideas, dreams, and aspirations. Only you can manifest abundance that could serve tens, thousands, millions, or even billions.

My books will last; they will be my legacy. Likewise, you have the wondrous potential to live your dreams, to create and contribute. It's only limited by your imagination.

ONE

What You Want Wants You

'd like to focus now on your purpose—also called mission statement, purpose statement, or unique selling proposition (USP), which I define as a destination with a deadline—and on your action strategy: what you will do specifically. This means a big goal broken down into doable daily parts. These parts need to be believable, achievable, specific, and meaningful to you. Big goals can be broken into bite-sized parts so you can easily accomplish a little each and every day. As the old joke says, how do you eat an elephant? One bite at a time.

To start with, ask yourself, "What do I really want, both personally and professionally?" As soon as this happens, you've engaged your conscious mind, and you'll start the ball rolling toward your desired results.

Now you could say, "I don't know what I want," so pretend the life of your kid or somebody that you really love is on the line: they will be vaporized if you don't know what you really want. You'll be amazed at how fast it will come to the forefront of your thinking.

Sometimes it also helps to say what you want out loud, hearing yourself replying, "I want this. I really want that." Clarity is power, and I'm trying to help you get clear.

I co-wrote a book called *The Power of Focus*, because focus generates magnificent results. Billionaire Warren Buffett says, "Clarity of focus made me billions." He also said, "In my mind's eye, without a computer or a notepad, I can remember and visualize a thousand different companies that I am personally interested in and at what price they would be a value buy-in for Berkshire Hathaway," which is his company.

Once you've got what you really want in mind, you've got to put it in writing, because, as I've already said, your conscious mind makes the decision and the subconscious mind will make the provision. But the subconscious can be devious. If your thoughts are full of fear or are even a little bit fear-ridden—I'd say, 1 percent doubt, and you're out—you'll be out of the picture, because all of us have some tricky little hidden fears.

The subconscious realizes this and gives you excuses for why it won't work. It'll trick you again, and pretty soon you'll forget about your goals, so you need to put them in writing.

For example, you can say to yourself, "I'm going to save 10 percent of my income, and I'm going to do it insistently, consistently, and persistently." But tomorrow, in the day-to-day rush of your life, the goal may seem to fade from memory; suddenly the subconscious has a free ride and forgets all about it.

Therefore, as soon as you set a goal, you need to put it in writing. My cliché is, "Don't think it, ink it." Write down this goal as a second act. It affirms that you have taken action, and it makes the action permanent. It becomes perfectly clear to the subconscious that we're not fooling around. This time we really intend to accomplish our goal.

It's important to note that you're really thinking about it, writing about it, or putting it in your journal. You are distilling it on paper, because when you write down a goal, you're committing your whole mind. The conscious and subconscious come together and will make your goal flow through with effortless effort.

It's easy to overlook a goal once we've just thought about it and it's flashed through our minds. Maybe we whispered it out loud. Maybe we told somebody about it and then quickly forgot it. It's a great deal harder to forget the goal if you get it in black-and-white, you deploy it on paper, and you look at it.

Many people will tell you to write down a goal, but I'm different from my peers. I tell you to write down too many goals. Don't just write down one or two goals. To start, I'm asking you to write down a dozen at least, and if you really hit my magic number, it's 101. Write down 101 goals.

Let me give you three reasons for writing down too many goals. First, different goals have different gestation rates. A chicken egg takes twenty-one days to break into life. A human embryo takes nine months. An elephant embryo takes two years. Goals are like that. Some are accomplished quickly, and some take a long time.

The second reason for writing down lots of goals: when they're reached, they lose their power and importance to you, and you enter into a mild to severe state of depression. So you need the next goal to go on to even before you get the last one. For example, if you wrote down that you want to get a new job and then you get one, that goal will become meaningless. It will lose its charm. It'll lose its spell on you. It's now worn-out. When you write down lots of goals, even though you accomplish some, there'll be plenty more to keep your subconscious mind at work.

The third reason that we're not limiting ourselves to just a few goals is the rule that the universe is abundant. Just when you think you've gotten everything you really want, why settle for less? Actress Mae West said it best: "Too much of a good thing is wonderful." You'll have a continuous sense of fulfillment and fulthrillment, with positive feedback forever reinforcing you. Personally, I've got over six thousand goals in writing, and it winds me up. Every day I get up feeling like Tarzan. I want to beat in my chest. I want to go into life with gusto, with zeal, with excitement. I'm titillated at the fiber of my being to go for the brass ring, so to speak, or the Holy Grail. If you have everything to gain and nothing to lose by setting all these goals, by all means try.

It's not that people want too much; it's that they want too little. The mind comes to work based on desire, backed with a do-it-now activity that reinforces and improves itself. Why not go for that gusto?

Once you have all these goals in writing, pair them off, like a eight-player tennis tournament. Keep pairing them off against each other and eliminating them until you are to down the last two. You will find the one driver, which, if accomplished, will fund and facilitate the accomplishment of all the other goals.

Twice a day for 365 days, once in the morning and once at night, write out that goal. That's 730 repetitions branded into your brain, the fabric of your being, and the soul of your belief system.

Compare that with what most people do. On New Year's Day, in the fog of a dreadful hangover, they write their annual goals and then proceed over the next few days to completely forget or neglect them.

I humbly and respectfully ask you to write down your goals. Take literally a minute or two to write out your goal first thing in the morning and last thing at night. You can see that this is more effective than doing it once every 365 days.

This process made Grant Cardone a social media and real estate billionaire. He's also a bestselling self-help writer and a speaking superstar who is still climbing and writing his personal goals twice a day.

This process works. Do what works. Begin at once, whether you are ready or not. You have everything to gain and nothing to lose. Keep doing it, and it will get easier and easier and you'll get better and better at it. Tell your family and friends to try it.

My friend Peter J. Daniel, the author of *How To Be Happy though Rich*, is the richest industrialist in Adelaide, Australia. He has a Rolls-Royce, a gold elevator in his office building, and a giant horse ranch. He has read and annotated over five thousand biographies and autobiographies of successful people and has connections to the who's who of the world. Peter says he'll never retire, because he's invested his entire life creating contacts, contracts, friendships, and resources. His master plan is completed on his eighty-fifth birthday, and then, he says, he goes into gear two. His wife, Robina, asked him, "With all your millions and millions, Peter, when will you retire?" He answered, "When you do, Robina. When you quit making the beds, loving the grandkids, and spoiling me rotten."

Don't compromise when you write down your goals. Your life's a story. Even so, life is not a dress rehearsal. You are in Life University every day, and your choice predetermines your future outcomes. Why not write your own glorious life story from the now through the end? Make it positive, happy, uplifting, and exalted, so that when your grandkids and great-grandkids look at it, they'll say, "Whoa. Grandma and Granddad really did something great. They made it happen, and so can I." Then go out and make it happen.

Ask yourself, what would you do with your life if you knew you could not fail? Put yourself in the mindset of an imaginative child. A child will ask for anything and everything without fear of rejection. Make it easy and fun. Put on the mindset of a twelve-year-old, because at twelve, kids think they know everything. You ask a twelve-year-old to write down ten goals in ten minutes, and they just do it. Get in that same flow. Do the first ten goals in ten minutes. You may be able to go beyond that, so go for it.

Your mission, should you choose to accept it, is to write down 101 goals. Write down short-term, intermediate, and long-term goals. As suggested earlier, the goals have to be definite, positive, specific, purposeful, and meaningful to one person only—you. Write down both the tangible and the intangible goals. Why not have love, romance, and peace of mind as intangible goals?

Your goals aren't written on a tablet, like the Ten Commandments and hidden in the Ark of the Covenant. You can change them and improve them, but just getting them on paper helps you look at them. Start with quantity first, then we'll improve the quality, and the clarity will also improve. My purpose is to be your source of inspiration in writing your goals.

Here are a few questions that might get you started. When you're a neophyte, it's best not to tell anyone about your goals. The reason is your new goals are like a newborn child. They're vulnerable and fragile. When you tell others—including your relatives—about your goals, they may just shoot holes in them. Don't ever do that. Keep your goals quiet in your soul. Only talk to friendly, like-minded people who have achieved some of their goals and who'll cheer you on and root for you.

I experienced this firsthand when my coauthor Jack Canfield and I released the first *Chicken Soup for the Soul* book. I said, "My goal is to sell a million and a half in a year and a half." When I said that we were going to create four best sellers in a year, the common answer was, "Yeah, right. You haven't even got one best seller, and you don't even have a publisher that will take you yet, but you're going to have an all-time best seller. Get out of here." Few people verbally supported my dream or Jack's, but we could see the end from the beginning, and we didn't let their doubts and disbeliefs get in our way.

Another example is my good friend Jeannie Harper. When she was in the fourth grade, her teacher asked her to write down her real goal—what she wanted to be when she would grow up. That night she went home and thought about it, because this was an important homework assignment to her. She came back happy, joyous, and exuberant, and handed in the paper. It said that she was going to be the first female commercial airline pilot in history. The next day she went skipping back to school, only to find that the teacher had given her an F and written next to it, "Unrealistic goal." It broke her heart, crushed her little spirit.

She went home and showed the paper to mom and dad. They said, "Jeannie, this is important, but whatever decision you make, we're going to back you 100 percent." She put back on her happy face, went in to the teacher the next day, and said, "You keep the F. I'm keeping my dream."

That's a good story, because it has even a happier ending. Jeannie was one of the first female commercial airline pilots for United Airlines and has done spectacularly well.

This is why in the beginning it's preferable not to share your dreams with somebody else unless you've got somebody that unconditionally loves you, supports you, and understands this process, and unfortunately there are only a few of us. Only about 3 percent of us are goal setters and goal getters.

I ask you to metaphorically step in there with me right now. Just decide in favor of yourself right now. Decide that you're going to be a magical, mystical goal setter for the rest of your life.

As you achieve more and more of your goals and begin to build a track record of success, tell the world about your goals, and others will emerge who can help you realize your aspirations, hopes, and desires. Once you start achieving your goals, and people see what you're doing, they'll start calling you outstanding, extraordinary, successful. They'll give you honors, plaudits, and trophies. The point is, do not invite discouragement early on by babbling about the goals you've set and what you plan on doing. Instead do it yourself, and let your results speak for themselves.

What's truly amazing is how fast you can emerge from the pack of maybes, I-hope-tos, and someday-ers into that small group of people who say, "I did it. Let's work together now and really accomplish something great and colossal."

When you achieve your goals, don't cross them out as you do when you go to the grocery store: "I got the milk. I got the eggs. I got the butter." I'm going to ask you to do something else. When you achieve your goals, write down, "Victory," because crossing your achievements off means that you won't get to look back at them. Instead you'll be looking at "Victory, victory, victory."

I suggest that you write "Victory" in purple or lavender, because those are the highest visible colors in the electromagnetic spectrum. They're at the top of the rainbow.

You'll start reinforcing yourself, saying, "Wait a second. I can really be victorious. I can go for this," because everyone's life has peaks and valleys. You need to be able to look back at your victories, put your right hand over your left shoulder, and say, "Attaboy," or "Attagirl." You can't let the valley get in the way of your peak achievement, because today's peak achievement is going to be tomorrow's valley.

If you write down too many goals, it's going to be exciting for you. Goals are for a lifetime. As I showed in the preface, fifteen-year-old John Goddard set his life's trajectory and more than accomplished most of it.

Goals are voluntary, not mandatory, but I'm going to ask you to make it a voluntarily mandatory assignment to set them. If you can speak to your spouse and talk him or her into it, great. If you can get your kids to do this on a regular basis, it'll wow you. Thomas Edison said it best. He said, "If you did what you were capable of doing, you'd astonish yourself."

Have a purpose—and a purpose that's bigger than you are. If you don't have any goals, your goal is to set some goals. If you don't have a purpose, your purpose is to have a purpose. Both your goal and your purpose have to be written out, preferably now, before you continue reading.

Things in themselves are indiscriminate and undirected. A leaf falls from a tree and is scattered with others in a heap on the ground, but leaves attached to a growing tree have a clear purpose of keeping that tree alive and healthy. Goals that are on purpose make your life dynamic, fun, enjoyable, and forever exciting.

Having an overriding purpose makes the difference in life. "A person without a purpose is like a ship without a rudder," said author Thomas Carlisle. Your purpose is the underlying direction that gives meaning to your goals. You may have hundreds of goals, some of which are going to be continuously achieving themselves and being outpictured as results, but your single purpose is how you're going to spend your life.

Let's expand on that a bit. A purpose is like the North Star. It's the guiding light that sets us on a course and keeps us fixed on it. Our minds need a purpose, or else we will wander, drift off, and accomplish little. Without a purpose, our achievements seem hollow, our future uncertain, and our present chaotic. With a purpose, everything falls into place. We suddenly have a basis for making life decisions. Thinking, reading, and other activities now become important and purposeful. You start to see things in your reading that you would have missed if you didn't have a driving purpose attracting you to it.

Determining our purpose therefore should be our first big mental task. In simple terms, it means being on purpose. You're doing what you love to do, what you're good at, and what's important to you; therefore it's going to be important to the world. Playwright George Bernard Shaw said it best: "The true joy in life is being used for a purpose recognized by yourself as a mighty one." Your greatest challenge is to discover and use your talents, resources, and abilities to their highest and best. The question is, what are your, or (in the first person) my talents, resources, skills, and abilities? How am I going to employ them at their highest and best— and get paid substantially for them? Our purpose in the Chicken Soup for the Soul series was to change and improve the world one story at a time. So far we have sold over a half billion books that have had a pass-along value of over two readers per book, so we have affected over a billion readers.

As I've read superstars' biographies and autobiographies, I've discovered a few self-revealed purposes. Ted Turner said, "I want to take CNN around the world." The first month he launched it, *The Wall Street Journal* said, "He hasn't got a chance." Ted has that article framed and hung in his office. Bill Gates said, "I want a computer in every home." It didn't seem possible at the time, but he partnered with Paul Allen, his boyhood best friend, and a genius as well. Together with Andy Grove at Intel, they made a computer that has gone from mainframe to desktop to laptop to smartphone.

Walt Disney wanted Disneyland and Disney World to be the happiest places in the world. His purpose was to make people happy, and I think he did. The late Princess Diana said she wanted to rid the world of land mines, which should be eradicated from the planet. She was photographed risking her life to find and destroy hidden landmines, which kill people every day. Despite her unfortunate death, she raised hundreds of millions of dollars for her goal. Mother Teresa said, "I am just a pencil in the hand of God." She wanted to alleviate the pain and suffering of the poor around the world, and her Sisters of Charity certainly got on about that business.

Henry Ford wanted to mass-produce and mass-distribute, and mass-market cars so they could be mass-consumed. He pulled off this passionate purpose, and changed the world from traveling in horse and buggies to automobiles, tractors, and trucks. John F. Kennedy set a purpose for the nation: "In this decade, we'll land a man on the moon and bring him safely back to earth." Isn't that a neat one? We did it, and now we are doing it again with free-enterprisers like Jeff Bezos, Richard Branson, and Back to Space, of which I am on the board of directors.

The Hunger Project, headed at the time by my friend Lynn Twist, author of *The Soul of Money*, raised over $15 million. The project is intended to alleviate hunger in a very short time, and it's done wonders: according to its website, it has reduced hunger by 33 percent in partner communities in Africa.

My purpose is to save lives, fortunes, and futures. My book *ASK! The Bridge from Your Dreams to Your Destiny*, coauthored with my wife, Crystal, is designed to help readers become master "askers" in order to fulfill their destiny. My book *You Have a Book in You!* is dedicated to inspiring everyone to think through, write, market, and share their valuable stories, thinking, and ideas with the world.

Once I was a commencement speaker at Life Chiropractic College in Marietta, Georgia. The oldest graduating doctor was seventy-two years young. (Never call yourself old. Always call yourself young. It's a good affirmation if you want to be ageless and timeless.) I hugged her, kissed her, congratulated her, and said, "Doc, before you came here to medical school, what did you do?" She said, "When I was sixty-five, I was a nun, and in my sisterhood, retirement was mandatory." I said, "Why? Why did you decide at that age to come back to school and invest seven years in becoming a doctor?"

She said, "Because I wasn't done yet, and I wanted to go out and heal people." She was powerfully on purpose.

We all need a purpose. We need to put it down in writing, so it's crystal clear, believable, and achievable. We should be able to say it with compelling conviction in seven memorable words or fewer.

If you don't have a purpose, as I've already pointed out, your purpose is to get a purpose. If you don't have goals, your goal is to get some goals. Make it your mission to discover your purpose and help others find theirs. I believe you were coded in your DNA and RNA with the purpose that you were supposed to realize, so a fulfilled life means you've got to be on purpose.

To find your purpose, I suggest that you go deep inside yourself. Use meditation and prayer to go to "the secret place of the Most High" (Psalm 91:1), cogitate, ruminate, and meditate. Have something to write with, and keep your pen poised. When the answer flashes, write it down, because as you look at it more and more, pretty soon you'll take ownership of it. You have the idea, and then the idea has you. Then you're going to be willing to share your goal, and you're going to have conquering power. You're going to be unstoppable, because you'll know what your purpose is, and you'll go out to make a difference and leave a legacy. It's all because you're willing to ask yourself in the quiet of your own mind.

Just before going to sleep, ask 101 times: "What is my purpose? What is my purpose?" Keep reiterating the same single question. It is the only way I know of into the innermost secret place of the Most High. Amazingly, an illumination will burst forth, probably in the middle of the night. Tell you sweetie or spouse that if you awaken at some strange hour, you will probably turn on the light and write down the most brilliant idea that you have ever had—one that will transform your life forever.

It's all because you're willing to ask yourself in the quiet of your own mind, "What is my purpose? What are my goals?" When you scribble them down, you're going to be amazed at how they start to unfold. It's going to be easy to write them down, because I've told you it's going to be easy, and if you believe it's easy, it's easy.

It's going to be even easier to start to achieve your purpose and goals. Once you get momentum, your momentum is going to have momentum. You're going to turn a lot of other people on to it. I'm so proud of you, and I want to say congratulations in advance.

If you were provided with absolutely everything you want and need to release your full potential and release your highest vision for yourself, what would your purpose be? That's what I want you to write down. I believe that you've got more than enough ability, and I want you to let it flow through you. Let it be effortless effort, have the wind beneath your wings, and go out and accomplish greatness.

TWO

Believe It and Achieve It

hope I've convinced you that by focusing your energy, you get more done in less time and achieve greater and more spectacular results. The technique I used to assist me in achieving my big goals is visualization. It goes by a lot of different names. Some people call it storyboarding, mind mapping, guided meditation, or picturizing. I don't care what name you use, but I'm sure you're going to like it once you learn and start to employ it.

First, we visualize what we want, and then we achieve it, because what we visualize, we realize. We see it in our mind's eye, the eye of our imagination.

We've got to visualize completely and repletely.

I think I can give an example of this: the *Titanic*, a luxury ocean-bound ship that was supposed to be totally unsinkable, but it hit an iceberg at 11:40 p.m. on April 14, 1912, and sank in the North Atlantic.

Decades later, cinematographer James Cameron said, "The story of the greatest ship of all time could easily become the greatest movie of all time." He got people to back it; its price tag surpassed anything that had ever been spent on a film up to that point—$200 million. The critics panned the idea. They said that the movie would sink; it was going to be an epic disaster about an epic disaster.

It doesn't matter what something costs; it matters how valuable it is. In the consumer mind, this movie was so valuable that people around the world lined up for tickets. At one point in Japan, people were in line at 7:00 a.m.

Cameron visualized the whole movie from the back to the beginning. He wanted an epic drama, a spectacular film, complete with unforgettable music.

The film *Titanic* is about a romance between a rich girl named Rose, played by Kate Winslet, who's traveling in first class, and a young, handsome, but poor boy who's traveling in steerage (the lowest cost way to travel), played by Leonardo DiCaprio. They have love but are separated by class distinctions. Cameron put them on a luxury liner and brilliantly showed everything that happened. You see the heroes deeply and indefatigably in love as they meet at the bow of the ship. Cameron even got the most improbable things, things that couldn't happen, into his mind's eye. He went through the picture, built it, and created the drama.

What do we learn from this? Cameron visualized the end result. He five-sensed his experience. He got us to feel it, smell it, touch it, taste it, experience every part of it as if we were really there. In the movie, there was love, terror, class struggle, grief, fear, tragedy, betrayal, a victim and victors, and people who blindly believed that the ship was unsinkable until the end of their lives. It was a perfect replication of a mental picture on the movie screen, so you understood the situation as intimately as somebody that had been on the boat. It reaches every one of your human emotions. When my daughter saw it, she said, "Daddy, I've got to go again and again."

Although the main characters are fictional, Cameron portrays events that actually occurred, and he gets us to believe him by simulating the *Titanic* experience with his cinematography. His power of portrayal gets us to understand what it must have been like to be on that ship on its maiden voyage. Jim and Suzy Cameron invited me to their home in Malibu for dinner, and we discussed this epic story. He was verbally as captivating and as exciting as he is visually in recounting what probably occurred that fateful night.

That's what I want for you. My goal is to have you learn to visualize the epic journey called your life. You start at the end, and you go backwards. You do it on an IMAX theater in your mind, showing you with a spectacular life and lifestyle, which gives you every good thing you want. Visualization works in the simplest things—getting better grades if you're a student. It works in getting a career or a promotion. If you're in the healthcare industry, it works in finding a medical breakthrough. It'll work for an Olympian, who can go from loser to winner if he or she visualizes.

In 1984, Carl Lewis told people that he was going to match Jesse Owens's historic record at the 1936 Olympics. He felt he would gain fame and fortune through endorsements. Well, Lewis got what he visualized. He equaled Jesse Owens's great records, but he got very few endorsement offers after the Olympics, and most people have already forgotten his name. In my opinion, the problem was that he visualized himself only matching Owens's record. Lewis should have visualized himself breaking through and setting a brand-new record. He could have instantaneously been known all over the world as an all-time Olympic record holder.

Perhaps the best example of visualization is my hero Walt Disney. Disney envisioned movies before they were ever filmed. He created a process called storyboarding—the art of creating complete story lines on art boards before the beginning of the movie. Walt was a master. He always saw the end before he even started putting his art pens to paper. He saw Disneyland in Anaheim, California, because he wanted an amusement park that was clean and attractive, with no gum on the pavement and no alcohol served. It would be great to go there.

Disney was a master at seeing. He saw the Experimental Prototypical Community of Tomorrow in Florida, known today as Epcot Center. He saw Disney World, Disneyland in Japan, and Disneyland in Paris, even though they weren't built until long after he died. When he was on his deathbed, a friend said, "It's a crime you're not going to see Disney World and Epcot finished, Walt."

He answered back without a blink: "If I didn't see it, you never will."

Walt visualized completely. He knew that it doesn't cost any more to dream big than it does to dream small. More clearly than anyone, he understood the power of visualization.

Jack Canfield and I work on many projects simultaneously, and we storyboard everything we want. We take a gigantic wall and we write down little yellow stickies with all our hopes, dreams, and desires. We put them up to create a wow of a business plan. We cut out the *New York Times* best-seller list. We cut out the name of whoever is number one and replace it with "Jack Canfield, Mark Victor Hansen, *Chicken Soup for the Soul*."

We visualized that result. We put it on the mirror, and we looked at it all the time, because the mirror technique goes right into your mind, through the portals of your soul, into the depth of your subconscious We had the idea, the dream, the visualization; then the idea, dream, and visualization had us. And you know what? Our successful visualization keeps happening; it keeps outpicturing.

Could you do the same thing or even more? You visually create your own world at a lot of levels. Your mind is 87 percent visual. Disney is reported to have asked his staff to be at work every day at 7:30 at his Burbank studios, point at their temples, and say, "My imagination creates my reality."

How right he was! The world we live in is the result of the imagination of all the people that put it there— the chairs, the glass, the windows, the cars. All those things were somebody's imagination that was realized. Our world is our imagination outpictured. We drive cars, live in houses, sleep in beds, have indoor plumbing. We can go to work easily and effortlessly in the morning in a car that's air-conditioned and comfortable, all because the natural order of the universe was inverted through our own wonderful human imagination. There was a time when those things didn't exist except in somebody's imagination. First they visualized these things, and then they worked collectively to realize them, so they now exist for you and me.

But why stop? Albert Einstein taught us that imagination is more important than facts. If we only use our minds instead of our behinds, there's no limits to where we can go.

Visualization is the process of seeing something within your mind before it actually happens. It's one of the most powerful principles available for creating your future. It converts sickness into health, fat people into thin people, losers into winners, poor people into rich people, unknown people into people who are beloved and famous.

Visualization even works to help governments turn their economies around. This fact was made apparent to me in the 1970s, when Abe Beame was mayor of New York. He seemed to lack both vision and the power of visualization. At one point he announced that New York City was going bankrupt. The story appeared on the front page of *The New York Times*, and it almost happened. That kind of thinking, visualization, and verbalization repels business, and it's a bad visualization. We don't need to be negative-minded or negative visualizers.

The mayor that followed Beame was Ed Koch. Koch said, "Business is great," and all of a sudden, business became great. The people who had left for Connecticut and New Jersey came back in droves.

Seven Steps to Creative Visualization

1. Relaxed awakeness.
2. Go into your imagination.
3. Come from the end result.
4. Change the past by reemotionalizing your life.
5. Five-sense your life.
6. An attitude of gratitude.
7. Take ownership of your visualization.

Relaxed Awakeness

There are seven steps to controlled visualization. Let's start with the first: *relaxed awakeness.* Sit on a comfortable chair, perhaps a recliner, or sit with your legs crossed effortlessly and comfortably, or lie flat on the bed. Listen to some upbeat background music that gets you into an alpha state of consciousness, such as Pachelbel's *Canon in D* or *Spectrum Suite* by Steven Halpern. This music goes at sixty beats per minute, which is the right pulsation and tempo.

Now you're positioned comfortably, you're doing this deep, resonant breathing, and you're getting centered and balanced. Put your right hand on your belly button, and breathe three fingers down from your belly button. Get into a centered, poised, relaxed awakeness, and breathe deeply. With this relaxed breathing, you're changing your state of consciousness.

As you breathe in, say, "I'm totally self-confident and self-assured and comfortable and relaxed." As you exhale, release everything that is unlike those qualities.

Go into Your Imagination

Step two: open your inner eye, *go into your imagination*, and visualize. In this stage, you decide to experience mastery. You see yourself as you want to be, doing what you want to do, having what you want to have, and going where you want to go. You might say such words as, "I see myself in the stage of my imagination. I see myself as strong and self-confident. I see myself driving to work effortlessly in the car of my heart's desire. I see myself going into my office (or practice or business) smiling, saying hello to everyone. As I walk in the door, I feel even the plush carpeting accept my feet. I see the original artwork on the wall, and the smells are just beautiful. I've got fresh flowers on every desk. Now I see myself going from meeting to meeting effortlessly, doing bigger and better deals than ever before, having more fun than I've ever had, and leaving work feeling more energized than when I came in."

Here you're imagining yourself as you want to be. You can do this at any level you want. Then you finalize it by saying, "I'm so thankful for that happy, exalted day."

The state of relaxed awakeness will bring you into the presence of the 3D imaging screen in your mind. Psychologists call this *associated visualization*, which means that you are in the picture; it is you in there.

Come from the End Result

Step number three: *Come from the end result.* The best example of this I can give you is Mary Lou Retton. Before she went into the Olympics, she worked with my colleague and friend Dr. Dennis Whitley, author of *The Psychology of Winning.* They wrote out one little three-by-five card. (I ask you also to write out your three-by-five card. See if you can do your whole visualization on one card.) Here's what she wrote: "I see myself going through every movement at the Olympics with effortless effort. I see myself coming off the high bars with my hands victoriously held high. I see Mama coming unglued out of her chair, with tears streaming down through her mascara. I see the audience giving me a tumultuous standing ovation. I see the digital clock reading out a perfect 10. I see a contract from Wheaties for $3 million."

Mary Lou had visualized the process in small steps, step by step. She saw it completely. She went over it over ten thousand times. She branded it into her brain and etched it into the fabric of her being, and she was there before she got there.

You can do the same thing: write down on the three-by-five card the experiences that you want tomorrow, next week, next month, at the end of the year, three years out, and visualize them to realize them. Come from the end result. Be where you want to be before you get there.

Jack and I visualized ourselves, not with a best seller but with a mega-best seller. Not just with a mega-best seller, but a mega-best-selling series. You may want to visualize yourself going to the college or university of your heart's desire. You may want to visualize yourself with a brand-new car. Go inside your mind's eye and go up to the new car you want. It's the color you always dreamed of. As you peer in, it's got the cushy seats that you were hoping for.

Now you open the door and you get in. It's got that nice, new car smell. You put your hands on the steering wheel and you feel the notches under your fingers. You look at the dashboard, and it's everything you ever dreamed of.

Now visualize traveling with the people that you want to travel with—your family, your loved ones, your future clients, whoever is going to be in that car with you. You see yourself parking, and you've got the status and the prestige you want.

It costs no more to have a great visualization than a crummy one. Why not just implode that into your mind so you explode into your realization and give yourself the car of your heart's desire, the job of your heart's desire, the home of your heart's desire?

Every architect, every interior designer is a master at visualization. Every professional does it in one way or another. Every athlete has to do it. All I'm asking you to do is go inside the video library of your mind and visualize from the end.

We started out by figuring out how to get into relaxed awakeness. Then we went into the theater of our minds, so we could see it, and now we're making the picture bigger and bolder.

Change the Past

We're expanding the frame. It's starting to absorb more of your mental cell tissue, and you're starting to think about it. We can go right into principle number four: *change the past by reemotionalizing your life.* Here's the good news: it's never too late to have a happy childhood. Your relationships with mom or dad or a teacher or a businessperson or employee, whether they were good or bad, are totally under your control. Those fragments of memory and imagination can be rewritten, reproduced, rescripted, and redirected, and you can have them the way you want.

Maybe the best example of somebody changing from lackluster to brilliant, shiny, and radiant is Shaw's play *Pygmalion*, which was later turned into the musical *My Fair Lady* (a movie that you can and must see on Amazon's streaming service). Here Professor Henry Higgins takes a girl that's being nothing, doing nothing, and having nothing and transforms her almost overnight into a lady. Hence the Pygmalion effect, which means that everybody can go from nowhere to somewhere great if they really want to.

There's another example of this; this is one is a true story and it's about Musashi. Musashi was the son of a samurai warrior in Japan. He was masterful at swordsmanship, but he didn't know how to be a good human being and did terrible things. He was ready to go off to jail, and they were ready to execute him. All of a sudden a Zen master came in and said, "Let me have him. Put him in my custody for three years."

For the three years, Musashi was in that man's custody. He was only allowed to read positive, uplifting, inspiring works. When he emerged after three years of this discipline, he was totally transformed. He became the greatest samurai of all time and the greatest contributor to Japanese society. The book *Musashi*, by the equivalent of our James Michener, is the most widely read book in Japan. It's sold over 120 million copies.

Now why do I tell you that? Because it's never too late to redirect your old thinking, which got you to the wrong place, and make new choices and rescript and redirect your life. What would happen if a million prisoners in America changed their input and automatically redirected their output? Don't let criminals watch TV and other things that will tread them down more, but let them read positive, uplifting, spirit-filled books that do good for them. It gives me goosebumps to think that we could get rid of crime in America.

I'll give the example of the Chicken Soup series. Not long ago we got a letter that said, "Dear Mark and Jack, I've been in the slammer five years, contemplating the ideal crime: killing the guy who put me here. My sister sent me your book. I've now read it six times, and when I get out of here in five years, I no longer want to kill the guy who put me here. I'm no longer violent to myself, other inmates, or the prison guards." Wouldn't it be neat if everyone had that change in input so they could change their output?

Five-Sense Your Life

The next one is *five-sense your life*. You've got five external senses: touch, smell, taste, hearing, and sight. Why not use the videos in your imagination to heighten every modality to its maximum impact? Use the IMAX theater inside the screen of your imagination. Color it with purple and live in the vibrant technology of our time. Use the Dolby sound or the Lucas surround sound of your mind's eye so you hear everything perfectly. Suffuse your olfactory sense. If you want to, you really can smell the rose or the lilac. Touch it, feel it, get the texture, get the grain. If it's edible, taste it.

Let me give an example. You go inside the best four-star Italian restaurant, and you start to salivate. You can smell the food already, even though it hasn't gotten close to the table. That's what I'm asking you to do. Visualize to realize your heart's desire by five-sensing it.

An Attitude of Gratitude

Point number six: have an *attitude of gratitude*. Be thankful in advance for all the good that you desire. The more you're thankful for, the more you get to be thankful for. Be thankful in advance for the prizes, rewards, windfalls, profits, bonuses, benefits, gifts, earthly angels, and friendships that you'll achieve.

The best example I can give of this is a janitor, forty years old, who was cleaning up a medical doctor's office on a regular basis. Over and over every night, he looked at the doctor's medical diploma on the wall.

One night, the doctor came back to the practice and saw the janitor ogling the diploma; he could see his name on it. The doctor said, "What is it that you want? You're the janitor here."

The janitor said, "I want to go to medical school."

So the doctor sat down with him. They went out for a cup of coffee, and he talked him through it. He helped the janitor get into a medical school. The guy later graduated, and his dream of dreams came true. He got to co-practice with the doctor who helped him transform himself from a janitor into a physician. (What diplomas do you see in your future?)

This janitor had it as his life's obsession to be thankful that he was going to become a medical doctor, and by the time he was fifty years old, he did. It doesn't matter what you want. It matters that you visualize from the end result.

Take Ownership of Your Visualization

Point number seven is *take ownership of your visualization*—every part of it so that your visualization and you become one. Jack and I visualized that we'd have a mega-best-selling series. Then we visualized all the branches it would take—a best-selling calendar, a perfect computer screen saver. We visualized a syndicated newspaper column for ourselves. We'd have cartoons and animation; we visualized being on TV.

This is how it turned out: for a while we had a column with King Features Syndicate. *Woman's Day* magazine paid us $4,000 a month for our articles. Vin di Bona, the famous owner and creator of American Home Videos, got us a show, and we had 1.2 million weekly viewers for three years.

It costs nothing to visualize, it's free. If you can visualize it, you can realize it. If you've fixed the thought in your visualization, I'll guarantee you a future realization, so you can literally live your dreams.

THREE

Positive Self-Talk

You are who you are because that's where you want to be. If you want to be somebody else or somewhere else, all you've got to do is change your self-talk and you'll change your future results.

The best example of this perhaps is Muhammad Ali, who may have been the greatest boxer in history. Before he received his acclaim, he was just another struggling fighter trying to break into the big time. At that point he was still Cassius Clay: he hadn't changed his name yet.

I certainly remember the headline on the sports page that quoted him as saying, "I am the greatest." Yes, he'd been great at the Olympics, but this claim seemed a little pretentious. At the time, the press scoffed at the young upstart. But he won, and they took notice. Not only did he win, but he predicted that he'd win. He began predicting the round in which he'd knock out his opponent. In all but two cases, he was right. He affirmed, "I dance like a butterfly, I sting like a bee. I'm going to KO you in round three."

How could Ali do that? He had tapped into a mysterious force that gave him the power to see into the future. That force is called *affirmation*. Affirmations are the words you say to yourself and others say to you that you believe, think about, and act on. Then these things come to pass.

Understanding affirmation: notice Ali never said, "I'm great," or "I'm almost the greatest," or "Next year, next month, or some other time I'll be the greatest." He simply and clearly stated, "I am the greatest," accomplishing three things simultaneously.

First, he let his own subconscious know what he had to work with, for the subconscious lives only in an eternal present, so he defined himself right here and now as the greatest. In effect, he was telling his subconscious what he was supposed to believe in the sweet now.

Second, by speaking his affirmation out loud and in front of others, he was putting his subconscious on notice that there's no backing down. He had declared it, and now he had to live up to it.

Third, once he lived up to it, he would become the world champion, and he got others to believe it as well. Thus when he said he would put another fighter away in the third round, he had to make sure the other fighter heard the declaration. That is psychological warfare at its best. When the third round came, the other fighter was waiting to be put away, and he got KO'd. Such was Ali's strength of affirmation that even other fighters believed it was going to happen. Consequently, it did. He psyched himself and other fighters out.

Ali also used other forms of affirmation besides the spoken word. Two of his other techniques were outstaring the opponent during the instructions before the match and never sitting down in the corner between rounds. These were kinesthetic affirmations that he was going to trounce them. They told him and his opponents that he was invincible and unstoppable.

Although Ali's boxing skills were indeed significant, even greater were his psychological skills. Ali was the ultimate boxer of the mind. All activities need to be won first in the mind and then in the battlefield.

The ultimate music affirmer of today may be country singer Garth Brooks. Garth is brilliant at music and marketing. As of late 2018, he'd already sold 78 million albums. He's en route to his self-espoused goal of outselling the Beatles' 100 million albums.

The important thing is, don't make any negative statements. An affirmation is a statement of belief. Without it, the subconscious is free to be programmed by others to what they believe. Since the subconscious is untrained, we also know what it believes whenever happens to be outpictured in our experience. It's like the robot R2-D2 in *Star Wars*. If it hears negative comments, it begins to think negatively. Then you become unsure and self-conscious, you withdraw, feel inferior, start to have low self-esteem, and grow helpless. You believe that, and then you start to act that way.

Likewise, positive thinking and positive believing cause positive results. It's the old law: cause + effect = result. Cause and effect are one, and the result is foreordained.

Too many of us only see the effects. We only see what the subconscious has wrought, not what it's doing. If things go wrong, if we lose, if we fail, we tend to look only at the effect. Most of us never realize that the cause is inside our own minds; the effect is what we see outside.

There's a movie I want you to rent and watch. It's called *Stand and Deliver*. It tells of a schoolteacher, Jaime Escalante. He taught in the ghetto in LA. One kid said, "I don't need to listen to you. See that Trans Am out there with the flames? That's mine. I earned it."

"No kidding. Where'd you earn it?"

"By working at McDonald's."

"Well, that's good for right now, but do you want to flip hamburgers for the rest of your life?" The kid was put in his place, stunned and willing to listen to a man of wisdom.

Escalante got the ghetto kids to start dancing calculus and doing math kinesthetically, and every one of them earned scholarships to Harvard, Wharton, Stanford, and Yale. It's a true story. With the music, plus a great, inspiring teacher and great, inspiring affirmations, the kids started believing in themselves positively and correctly and achieving positively and correctly. Any one of us can do the same thing. As Napoleon Hill, author of *Think and Grow Rich,* said, "Whatever the mind can conceive and believe, it can achieve."

In order to achieve your goals, you've got to believe that you can do it. Just giving lip service won't do. You've got to take action, because action proves your belief. As I've already pointed out, beliefs determine our actions, and actions determine our results. You've got to do massive right thinking and take massive right action in order to get massive right results here and now.

Consciously believing is the key to consciously achieving, but how do we arrive at our beliefs?

As I've already suggested, we need to put our goals in writing. We need to visualize the goal. Now we need to affirm it, to drive it home, to embed it deep in our mind's experience. Affirmation is a key that unlocks the door to belief. Humorist Will Rogers used to say, "I only know what I read in the papers." Although he said that as a joke, it's true that we tend to believe the things that are written down.

Moreover, we all tend to believe something that's been affirmed again and again. If it's repeated, pretty soon it gives itself credibility. When we say it out loud, especially when you have an audience of at least one, our own subconscious starts to buy into it. When our subconscious hears us affirming something, we start to give it the benefit of the doubt. The mind starts to say, "Maybe he's right," When we affirm it in front of somebody else, we really start to put the squeeze on our subconscious. It says, "Wow. You really did say that. You've committed yourself. If you don't follow through now, you'll look like a fool, and you'll be embarrassed. Now I have to get off my behind and save you in this thing. I'm going to make my mind go to work and get this done for you."

Do you see the power of affirmation? It forces your subconscious to believe that you really can do it. The question is how. There's vital importance in affirming and achieving our future greatness and living up to our potential, but how do we do the affirming?

At first, you may want to state your affirmations alone until you get the hang of it. Later on, you'll probably feel comfortable enough to make them in public.

The first thing you must do is stand. Standing brings you to full, conscious attention. I always suggest that people stand whenever they're doing something important—for example, making a telephone call that matters. The next time you're on the phone, instead of sitting down and letting your energy go down, stand up and listen to yourself. Even record yourself and listen to it and analyze it. Your voice and energy have to be up to empower your newfound brilliance and enthusiasm. A lot of times when you can make an affirmation, you've got to back it with other words.

Next, make a statement of the affirmation. Make it loud. Make it clear. Be sure that your voice isn't quivering. Mean it. Once in a while I say to my audiences, "How's business?" I teach them to say, "Booming!" and they say, "Booming." I say, "You don't believe it, so you can't achieve it. Now give it to me in your outdoor kid-like voice," and they shout, "Business is booming!" If you talk, think, act, walk, and affirm that business is booming, pretty soon, believe it or not, it'll be booming, because business is always booming for someone, somewhere, somehow, some now. Why don't you affirm that business is booming for you?

In the Star Wars sequel *The Empire Strikes Back*, Yoda, the Jedi teacher, tries to implant in Luke Skywalker the means of engaging the Force, the greatest power in the universe. Yoda says, "Luke, there is no try. Either you do or you don't do." The Force is the felt power of affirmation. You make it so by saying that it's so, believing that it's so, and achieving that it's so. These are simple words, but they have a world of meaning.

When you say something like, "I'm going to try to be the greatest," or "I'm going to try to be beautiful," or "I'm going to try to succeed," the "try" weakens you. It demeans you. It takes you to mediocrity. Why not go for the greatness? Affirm something positive, simple, elegant, in the present tense—because the future tense doesn't work in the subconscious mind—and do it with conviction, because if you're convinced, you're convincing. In the privacy of your own car or house or bathroom, you may want to shout it. Go for the loudness. Blow the lid off. Get the message deep inside your subconscious.

The next part is, you've got to do it often. The more you affirm, the sooner your subconscious will become obedient, go to work, and get the results that you've been affirming. Touch yourself and say, "I feel healthy. I feel happy. I'm a genius, and I'm learning to apply my genius." Jab yourself in the chest. It anchors the thought, to use a term from neurolinguistic programming.

So far we've talked about how and when to affirm. The next logical step is ask, "What should I affirm?" This, of course, is a personal choice. It depends on your purpose and your goals. I suggest that you have a main affirmation to constantly repeat as well as other little affirmations on the side. You create your own main self-affirmation. Go for something that's simple, positive, succinct, and constructive. It should be easy to repeat, so it becomes like a perpetual, continuous loop in the recordings of your mind.

When you've created your self-affirmation, start doing it the first thing in the morning. Do it when you get out of bed. Stumble to the mirror and look at yourself. At first talking into the mirror is going to be a little disconcerting, but as you do it a few times, you get better and better.

Let's talk about it. You're going in front of that mirror. You've just woken up. Your hair's disheveled. You have no makeup on. If you're a man, maybe you have a growth of beard. You haven't brushed your teeth yet, so you still have what TV calls green breath. You've got wrinkle lines from your pillow impressed on your face, and you go, "Ugh."

It's easy to go downhill from there and succumb to negative input. So program something positive, like "I feel healthy, I feel happy, I feel terrific." Beat on your chest if you really feel good about yourself. Say "I love you, positively and correctly. Today you're going to go out in the world. You're going to make a difference."

Now monitor your reaction. At first you're going to be amazed at yourself. You may tell yourself, "You're crazy," but that's negative programming. I'm asking you to choose to be happy. Affirm to yourself, "I feel healthy. I feel happy. I feel terrific. I feel successful. I feel prosperous. I love others, and others love me, positively and correctly. I am succeeding with everyone I meet. All my results are having positive results. My life is in perfect flow. My results are clicking." At that point maybe you want to click your fingers.

Choose to brighten your day with one of the oldest techniques known. Smile in the mirror, because you know that when you smile at somebody, they smile back. So start the day with a smile and say to yourself, "Good morning. I love you. We're going to have a great day. I'm going to make it terrific." Be your own cheerleader. Be your own rooting commission. If you don't totally like your face, remember what we learned from Maxwell Maltz, the psychiatrist, plastic surgeon, and author of *Psycho-Cybernetics*. He said that as a plastic surgeon, he could make somebody beautiful, but if they didn't affirm, "You are beautiful," they would see themselves as ugly or disfigured as they had been before the operation. While his patients were still in gauze and couldn't look at themselves, he had them affirm, "You are beautiful."

Without having surgery, tell yourself, "You are beautiful," or "You are handsome," or "You are lovely." If you do that while you're still in the shower, you're going to give yourself a glow of zest from the inside out, and you're going to roar out of the shower like a lion or a lioness. Repeat this again in front of your mirror in the privacy of your bathroom. Say it quietly if you fear others are near, out loud if you are alone.

After you've learned to affirm yourself, the most important people you can affirm are your children. Let me give you an example.

Once my little daughter Melanie came home from school and sat at our evening family powwow at dinner. All of a sudden she burst into tears and said, "Mommy and Daddy, you don't understand. My best friend, Sarah, is no longer my best friend. She's now Megan's best friend, and I don't have any friends, and I'm outside of her clique." I was amazed that she knew the word *clique*.

My wife and I talked to her for two hours about this. We said, "Honey, this is why we've taught you how to do these affirmations and say, 'I love me, positively and correctly.' This is why we've said that you want to make yourself your best friend. Mommy and daddy are your best friends. As much as I love Sarah, Sarahs are going to come and go, but if you are self-affirmed and you feel good about yourself from the top down and inside out, you'll be able to handle it."

She started feeling good, and I said, "Look. My parents couldn't do what I'm going to do for you, but I'm going to call Sarah's parents and talk to them about having Sarah become your best friend again. I can't promise you that it'll work. Maybe it will, maybe it won't. The other thing I'm going to do is I'm going to call your teacher, because at the fourth grade, you start to fade in and out of relationships. I'd like you to be bonded in a relationship, because you want to be. I'm going to affirm Sarah, I'm going to affirm your teacher, and we're going to see that it happens."

For some reason, I'm blessed to say that it worked. Melanie's best friend became Sarah again.

Even so, relationships will come in and out of your life. If you feel good about yourself, you can handle the pulsations of life, the ebbs and the flows, the goods and the bads, the compliments and the condemnations. We can handle all the greatness that happens as well as all the critics that try to lambaste us. It is imperative to stay positively and correctly self-affirmed so you can affirm those that you love most—your spouse and your children.

Once you've really gotten good at affirming yourself, you can go out and affirm others. It costs nothing to do, yet it pays dividends that are profound. When you affirm another being, you raise his or her self-esteem. The other person will reciprocate in turn, and you'll receive bountiful rewards, maybe not directly from the person you're affirming, but overall. If you keep putting the universe in your debt, it comes back to you, and it'll flood you with niceness. I promise you I'm the beneficiary of such an experience.

If you're sincere, honest, and genuine, the simplest and most favorable way of influencing others is to use affirmations and compliments. Before I compliment a person, I ask, "May I have the right to pay you a compliment?" A lot of people have such low self-esteem that they'll reply, "No. Not me. You couldn't mean it." Nonetheless, there's virtue in doing this.

Now you can't compliment everyone on their mental or physical attributes, because you'd be accused of being insincere, but there's another way to pay a compliment that no one can deny: go for the person's core set of qualities and beliefs. Are they funny? Sincere? Courageous? Disciplined? Well-organized? Loving? Compassionate? Dedicated or persistent? Compliment their behavior. You're almost always safe in doing this. You say, "You're the person that emanates the highest level of integrity that I've ever seen." Maybe it's morality, ethics, or honesty—whatever it is, be straightforward. "You're the best risk taker I've ever seen." Or, "You're somebody who really cares about animals. I've never seen anyone that had such compassion for animals or children."

When we affirm these qualities and beliefs in somebody, we're acknowledging them to the core of their being. This is the deepest, most powerful kind of affirmation we can give to another person. A person that has succeeded at a project, a child that has learned how to ride a bike, or a friend that has learned how to be an expert skier—when we affirm all these people in their accomplishments, we add to their self-esteem. Mark Twain once said, "One good compliment can last me two weeks. Oh heck," he added, "some compliments are so good they'll last me a lifetime."

Affirm everyone you meet. Say something nice to them. It'll help them immensely. It'll come back to you in many positive and often unseen ways.

I've gotten lots of compliments over my lifetime. If they come from somebody you care about, they live with you. They go into the marble of your mind. They go onto the big screen. When you need them most, you'll be able to pull them out.

I ask you to be a compliment giver who's sincere, genuine, and honest. What results are you going to get? True affirmations, along with writing down your goals and using the power of visualization and verbalization, will give you amazing results. How amazing depends on each of us individually.

Affirmation is just another technique to help you change your belief system, your assumptions, and your perceptions about the most important person in the world—you. It allows us to harness those eighty-six billion brain cells and drive them where we want to go, so that we can get singularly and passionately on purpose and have a connection to our higher self. You will engage your subconscious and transform yourself from the inside out. You'll get to use the Pygmalion effect in a positive and correct way.

If you really do a good job transforming yourself, then, like Jaime Escalante, you can transform others. You can take losers and make them into winners, because they're going to believe in you as their coach, their guide, their mentor.

These little affirmations are invisible, and it doesn't hurt to have them. Why not share them? Once you become accustomed to the process, you'll find out that it's really quite elementary, and you'll be able to do it with increasing frequency and facility.

Let's say that your belief about yourself is that you're unattractive and you have difficulty making friends. Let's change the belief: start telling yourself, "I'm attractive in all ways and in all situations, and it's effortless effort for me to have friends. I like myself positively and correctly. I like myself alone, and I like myself with other people. My friends have friends. I like them, love them, respect them, and admire them, and they love, like, respect, and admire me."

Key number one is to change the process by setting a goal. Write down a goal or goals. By so doing, you make it crystal clear in your mind. Then you visualize the goal completed. You use the seven steps that were laid out in the previous chapter.

Next, the affirmation is aimed at the end result. Before you go to sleep, play back a series of affirmations. "I am lively. I am lovely. I'm outgoing. I'm friendly. I'm poised. I'm charming. I am meeting people who are instantly attracted to me. I am having the time of my life. My life is so good that I should be two people to experience all this good."

Repeat these affirmations every night before you go to sleep. Practice them for a month until they become automatic, until they're woven into the fabric of your being.

If you will, write down too many goals. Visualize them, verbalize them, and feelingly believe them. You'll not only achieve them but will get to live your dreams.

FOUR

Turning Problems into Assets

Life is a grindstone, and whether it grinds you down or polishes you up is up to you and you alone to decide.

—CAVETT ROBERT

D r. Norman Vincent Peale was walking down a street when a young man walked up to him, grabbed him by the lapels, and said, "Please, please help me. I can't handle my problems. They're just too much."

Dr. Peale said, "Look. I've got to go give a talk. If you let go of my lapels, I'll show you a place where there are people with no problems."

The man said, "If you could do that, I'd give you anything. Please do it."

"It's two blocks from here," said Dr. Peale. "But you may not want to go there once you see the place."

They walked over to Forest Lawn Cemetery. Dr. Peale said, "Look. There are 150,000 people in there. I happen to know that none of them has a problem."

Dr. Peale never tired of telling that story, which illustrates the true nature of problems. Problems are a sign of life, but they can be assets; they can be assets to your ascent. If you have a problem, big or little, be thankful for it. It proves that you're alive and functioning. In fact, some say that the best way to judge a person is by the size of his or her problems.

Most people, of course, believe problems are bad. They feel that the ideal state of things would be a problem-free existence; therefore, if they have a problem, they think something must be wrong. As a result, they devote a large part of their energies to bemoaning their fate.

In fact, our big problem may be somebody else's little problem. It's all a matter of perspective and applying new, creative, innovative solutions. To a child, a ten-pound suitcase may be heavy. To Arnold Schwarzenegger, it's probably so light that he can lift it with one finger.

We end up saying to ourselves, "Everything will be great if only I didn't have all these problems." That's the pessimist's lament. The optimist, on the other hand, sees problems as opportunities.

Author and insurance magnate W. Clement Stone was known for saying, "Problems are good! I thank God I have problems. Problems are what help me grow and get stronger." If you've faced a severe problem and broken through your fears in dealing with it, you'll immediately know what he's talking about.

Stone coauthored books with Napoleon Hill. They said, "Every adversity has a seed of equivalent or greater benefit." You may not see it immediately, but if you look deeply into your problem, you will, although it may require meditating deeply or changing your perception completely to find your answer.

To inspire yourself, consider making a list of all the problems you've successfully solved. Most of us haven't done that. As a result, most of us can't buy into the belief that problems can be opportunities in disguise. After you do this exercise, you will start to understand that most problems are solvable. If you're alive, you will have problems. Problems are a sign of life, as Dr. Peale observed above. You have obviously solved many, or you would not be here.

Since I can't reach out and talk to you personally about your problems, I'm going to do the next best thing. I'm going to discuss several people who have had incredibly severe problems and have gotten amazing results from them. Let's take four areas that people tend to worry about most: finances, physical appearance, multiple losses, and poor health.

Back from Bankruptcy

Let's start with financial problems, since most of us can easily relate to them. I am my own best example here. Back in 1974, I was just twenty-six years old. I was building $2 million a year worth of geodesic domes in New York City. Geodesic domes, you may recall, are triangles linked together to form large, inhabitable units that turn into spheres. They were invented by my mentor and great friend, Dr. R. Buckminster Fuller. It's one of the most famous of his many major patents.

At the time I was selling domes as fast as I could make them. I built the Wall Street Racquet Club, lion cages, aviaries, and many houses in New York City and the Catskills, but I had a problem. This was the year of the Arab oil embargo, and I was making domes out of polyvinyl chloride, PVC, a petrochemical plastic-based product. It was definitely the wrong time to be doing that. When OPEC was formed, the price of oil products shot through the roof, and the Arabs said, "We can write checks so big we'll make your banks bounce."

It seemed as if one day I was on top of the world, and on the next day I heard the judge saying, "Mark Victor Hansen, you are hereby declared bankrupt."

On the courthouse stairs before my trial date, a young attorney was soliciting me to take my case. "Use my services," he told me. "For $300, I'll file bankruptcy for you." I said, "Pal, if I had $300, I wouldn't be going bankrupt." To handle the case, I actually had to check out a book at the library: *How to Go Bankrupt by Yourself*.

That was my all-time lowest hour. I was so low, I had to reach up to touch bottom. On the scale of one to ten, I was a minus twelve. I got physically sick and felt like throwing up. Tears rolled down from my eyes, and my ears were temporarily blocked. I felt rejected and dejected, and I totally objected, both personally and professionally. I climbed deep within my shell— permanently, I thought. I had to lock out the world. I was afraid that everybody knew I'd gone bankrupt and was a total failure. My escapist behavior included sleeping nearly round the clock. I went to bed at 6:00 p.m., lying to myself that I was tired, and got up again at 6:00 a.m.

I was bummed out. I tended to think of it on the humorous side, though. Just after going bankrupt, I parked my little car, a beat-up Volkswagen, in New York's Pan Am Building. They valet who retrieved my car looked at me standing there, with the only suit the bankruptcy courts had left me with, and said, "Man, I would have picked you for a Cadillac." I said, "Me too."

I went from up to down in no time flat. Suddenly I was driving around, as I said, in a $400 permanently air-conditioned Volkswagen with pitted windows. In the geodesic dome business, I was a salesman, an executive, and a white-collar man, and now I said, "Who am I?" At that time I misunderstood, thinking my net worth and self-worth were the same.

I hit bottom. During my lowest days, I would drive my junk heap into service stations, and they'd say, "Fill her up, mister?" I'd say, "Twenty-five cents will do, thank you." I was embarrassed, but they were patient. Perhaps they could feel my predicament.

With my self-esteem completely trashed, I was at the bottom, but being at the bottom was a turning point, my time of greatest opportunity. I learned the principles of sharing and teaching. One key is, no matter how bleak things are, never, never, give up. There's always a way to solve every problem. It's so critical that I want to repeat it, and I want you to really think about this: *there's always a way to solve every problem.*

After that, things couldn't get any worse for me. Everything from there aimed up. That's an important message, and too often I missed it. We tend to look down on people who have gone bankrupt, but in reality, at that point the world is totally open to them. They don't have to cling to any job they don't like, any business that doesn't fit them, or any financial arrangement that traps them. They have 360 degrees of freedom. They can choose from over 37,000 occupations in America. The world is suddenly wide open to them, and everything is pure potential. If you listen to individuals who have overcome their failures, setbacks, and upsets, you will start to believe in yourself again. Like the phoenix in Greek mythology, you can rise from the ashes.

As I rebuilt my self-worth by listening to self-help audios, I quickly regained my net worth and created a new network of friends, clients, and customers. From being bankrupt that I could move up all over again. This time, however, I learned and lived by the principles I'm teaching in this book. A friend told me later, "Mark, you burned your bridges behind you. You had to succeed."

Today, I have a lovely wife, two beautiful daughters, an estate in Southern California, and a second home in Kona, Hawaii. I travel over 100,000 miles a year, having brought my message of hope, love, courage, and support to millions of people throughout my career.

I don't say all this to brag about myself but to show you that if I can do it, you can. Even I can turn my life around from poverty to plenty, from lack to lots, loads, abundance, and plenty.

The very bottom, financially speaking, turned out to be a nice place to start the rest of my life. I was resilient. I bounced back. I don't care what's happening in your life. You can still bounce back. You are resilient and can overcome all the obstacles before or behind you.

I had thought I had a problem, but it was really an opportunity in disguise. Going bankrupt was (given the insight of hindsight) my best worst experience, because it got me out of building domes, which I shouldn't have been doing, and into professional speaking, writing, promoting, marketing, and being an entrepreneur and a stimulator to awaken people to their own inner abilities. This is what I should have been doing, and am doing. It is my vocation, my unique talent, my superpower. Up to that point I had been living someone else's dream—Buckminster Fuller's.

The question is, what is your superpower? Believe me, you have one or more. If we meet at one of my future seminars, although I can listen to you for only a scant few minutes, I'll tell you what it is, as I have done for countless others.

The other way to discover your superpower is get a mastermind partner and together read out loud each question from my book *ASK! The Bridge From Your Dream To Your Destiny*. Listen to each other, record your answers in writing, and then discuss them. Voilà! Your superpower will be discovered.

Let me repeat: each of us has a unique talent. We just need to discover it. Consider asking positive and encouraging friends to tell you *how* you are unique and talented. Write down what they say, and if you think you have financial problems, put them in perspective. They may be trying to tell you something. Ten years from today, you may be looking back and seeing that they were in reality a tremendous life-changing opportunity. Allow me to persuade you that you can achieve wealth and financial freedom and become debt-free, stress-free, and financially free.

At his first job interview, Walt Disney was told that his drawings were amateurish and he lacked ideas—hardly an appropriate judgment. The line is, "Judge not by appearances." Winning is absolutely available to you if I can persuade you that it is and you start to believe that you can achieve it.

Financial difficulties are the most likely ones for people to encounter sometime in life. They may seem severe as we are experiencing them, but in truth, they are the mildest and easiest of problems to solve, After all, financial difficulties can generally be resolved by something rather simple and obvious—more money.

Becoming Beautiful

Other problems are more intractable. Take, for example, looks. Physical attractiveness or its opposite, ugliness, is of almost universal concern. I think more people worry about their physical appearance than about anything else about themselves. They consider it to be their biggest problem. Haven't you ever been concerned about your own physical attractiveness? Perhaps you were a teenager or even an adult with blemishes. Haven't you ever felt that maybe you didn't look quite as good as you should? It may be something as simple as a bad hair day or clothes that in daylight turn out not to match.

Haven't some of your life decisions been based on how you feel about your appearance? Haven't some of those decisions acted to hold you back, even just a little? What if at age forty-six, you're burned beyond recognition in a terrible motorcycle accident, then four years later were paralyzed from the waist down in an airplane crash? Can you imagine yourself becoming a millionaire, a respected public speaker, a mayor of your hometown, a happy newlywed, a successful businessperson? Can you see yourself going whitewater rafting and skydiving?

My friend and fellow speaker and author W Mitchell has done all those things after two horrible accidents that left his face a quilt of multicolored skin grafts, his hands fingerless, and his legs thin and motionless in a wheelchair. Mitchell endured sixteen surgeries after his motorcycle accident, which had burned over 65 percent of his body and left him unable to pick up a fork, dial a phone, or go to the washroom without help, but Mitchell, a former Marine, never believed he was defeated. "I'm in charge of my life," he said. "It's my up or my down. I choose to see this situation as I want to. It's a starting point, and I'm starting my life over."

Six months later, he was piloting a plane again. Mitchell was back on the road to success. He bought himself a beautiful Victorian home in Colorado, some income-producing real estate, an airplane, and a bar. Later he teamed up with two friends and cofounded a wood-burning stove company that grew to be Vermont's second-largest private employer.

Exactly four years after the accident, the plane Mitchell was piloting crashed back into the runway during a takeoff, crushing Mitchell's twelve thoracic vertebrae and permanently paralyzing him from the waist down.

"I wondered what the hell was happening to me," he asked. "What did I do to deserve all this?" Undaunted, Mitchell worked day and night to regain as much independence as possible. He was elected mayor of Crested Butte, Colorado, and saved the town from mineral mining that would ruin its beauty and environment. Mitchell later ran for Congress, turning his odd appearance into an asset with slogans such as "Not just another pretty face."

I love, respect, honor, and appreciate this guy, and I am glad to call him my friend. Despite his initially shocking looks and physical challenges, Mitchell began whitewater rafting. He fell in love and happily got married. He expanded his education and earned a master's degree in public administration. He continued flying, is involved in environmental activism, and is a phenomenal public speaker who wakes up every audience member to their true inner beauty. You can watch him on YouTube.com and see his presentation "It's Not What Happens to You!"

Mitchell said, "Before I was paralyzed, there are ten thousand things I could do. Now there are nine thousand left. I can either dwell on the thousand I lost or focus on the nine thousand I have left. I tell people that I have two big bumps in my life. If I could choose not to use them as an excuse to quit, then maybe some of the experiences you have can pull you back and give you a new perspective. You step back, take a wider view, and maybe say it isn't such a big deal after all. Remember, it's not what happens to you, it's what you do about it."

I suggest that your concept of your physical appearance need not block you. You don't have to pity yourself. It has nothing to do with choosing to live an extraordinary life.

W Mitchell's experience gets each of us out of our pity parties and "ain't it awful" stories. When asked what W stands for, he gets a big smile on his face and says. "Wonderful!" Note: your appearance is wonderful in many ways, and being grateful will make it even better.

Defeat Defeatism

Some people say, "I'm a loser." A great many of us have defeatist attitudes. Usually it's because we've been put down so long that we start to believe it's normal and natural to be put down. In fact, we start to expect it, look for it, and even stimulate it to happen to us. We can't win because we think we are proverbial born losers, Calamity Janes or Calamity Jims.

A tattoo artist once told me that his best-selling tattoo was "Born to Lose." What a horrible affirmation to make for yourself, especially to view it for life on your arm or your leg. Worse still, I have seen it on someone's forehead. I believe we need to tattoo on our minds that we are born to win, to live our dreams. Henry Ford said, "Whether you think you can or whether you think you can't, you're right."

Once we define our problem as being a loser, how can we possibly win? We've eliminated any possibility of success, but having previously lost isn't the problem. It's how we view our losses. It's not what happens to us, it's how we react to what happens to us. An optimist might say that we just haven't succeeded yet.

Perhaps the most universally acclaimed example of this principle is Thomas Edison. Edison didn't always enjoy the acclaim and respect in which we hold him today. When Napoleon Hill went to interview the great Edison for the first time, he said, "Mr. Edison, what have you got to say about the fact that you failed ten thousand times in your attempts to create the light bulb?" Edison replied, "I beg your pardon? I never even failed once. I had ten thousand learning experiences that didn't work. I had to go through those learning experiences to find the way that did work."

We all have had thousands of learning experiences, like learning to walk. When babies learns to walk, they fall, but undaunted, they get up and go at it again, until walking success emerges as normal and natural. We keep trying because we've seen others succeed. It's not that we are two- or three-time losers; it's just that we haven't had enough learning experiences to get it right yet. After someone has had a stroke, it takes eighty repetitions of lifting a glass to the mouth again to get it perfect every time. Many of us, if we just have one experience that it doesn't turn out positively, conclude we're losers and give up.

Most of us are too hard on ourselves. "I just can't do that" is a common lament. Is it valid? To say that we can't succeed because we failed once, twice, or more in the past is nothing more than the expression of fear that we'll fail again. As long as we have that fear, it's a roadblock that's going to be thrown up against us.

This is the time to pull out the stops for yourself and others. Encourage yourself, and encourage others. Do it now. Create a space of new possibilities for yourself and everyone else. We've seen it with Edison, and we can see it with you.

When Jack and I wrote *Chicken Soup for the Soul*, we thought we could do it in three months. It took us three years. It was an act of love, courage, and devotion. We got a great agent to go with us to New York. With our agent, we went to thirty-three different publishers. All of them said, "Get out of here. Nobody buys short stories, and that title is too nicey-nice." Ultimately our book was rejected 144 times. Then our agent fired us.

Producer Peter Guber, who has Academy Awards for films such *Rocky*, *Batman*, and *Rain Man* and is owner of the Golden State Warriors and Los Angeles Dodgers, likes to jokingly tell everyone, "Mark is so dyslexic, he thinks *no* means *on*." I am not dyslexic at all, but I reject rejection and keep at whatever I want until I succeed and complete my magnificent purposeful obsession— my destiny.

All of us get rejected. The way to handle it is to keep saying mentally, "Next. Next. Next," because in life you don't get paid for your success, you get paid for your confrontations en route to success.

When H. Ross Perot was working for IBM in 1962, he made $287,000 in the first seventeen days. That was his yearly quota, so he didn't have to work for the rest of the year. Fascinated with the idea of servicing computer software, he brought his idea to IBM, but they weren't interested. He borrowed $1,000 from his wife, started a new company called EDS—Electronic Data Systems— and went out and started on knocking on doors. Eighty out of eighty prospects said no. The eighty-first person said yes and gave him a $4 million net commission. You divide 4 million by eighty, and you find that Perot got paid $50,000 every time he said, "Next." Is "next" a word you want to have in your vocabulary in order to handle your own and others' rejections? Rejection can pay brilliantly well if you can handle it.

Overcoming Illness

Next excuse is, "I'm too sick." I hope that as we've gone through this, I've started to strike a chord within you, showing you that we need to get rid of our excuses, the excuses that force us to defeat ourselves. In life, you either have excuses or results.

I'm sure that you can relate to this next story. It deals with sickness. I'm not talking here about a hypo-chondriac who only believes that he or she is physically sick and is really just escaping from reality. That's a problem of false evidence appearing as real, but it's not nearly as devastating as one faced by somebody who's truly ill.

I believe we must maintain physical health if we are to keep our lives in balance rather than being distracted from our goals by a physical body that is dragging us down. Health problems can strike at any age. Do we languish in our discomfort and our fear of staying sick, or do we break through and continue to seek achievement and greatness?

The late actor Christopher Reeve appeared in stellar movies like *Somewhere in Time*. His most famous role was that of Superman, who was always fighting for truth, justice, and the American way. Christopher was also a superstar athlete, and, among other things, a champion equestrian. One day in 1995, he was out riding. While he was doing an elementary jump, his horse suddenly stopped, and somehow his hands got twisted up in the reins. He went over the top. He went straight down on his head and broke his spinal column. Luckily there was a doctor, an anesthetist, not far away, who came and untied him and got him to breathe again.

As Christopher realized he was totally paralyzed and couldn't get up, he said to himself, "Do I want to end it all?" His three-year-old son came over, kissed him, and said, "Daddy, I love you." He immediately turned it around and said, "I'm here to make a difference."

At the hospital, they gave him the bad news that he was going to be a quadriplegic for the rest of his life, but as he recovered, he worked strenuously toward rehabilitation. He became a film director and continued to appear in films, winning a Screen Actors Guild Award in 1998 for his role in a remake of Alfred Hitchcock's *Rear Window.*

Later he became a spokesperson for the people incarcerated in wheelchairs and used his celebrity status to draw attention to spinal cord injuries. He was elected chairman of the American Paralysis Association. He became an activist on behalf of innovative rehabilitation and did a tremendous amount of good work until his death in 2004.

When you listened to Christopher Reeve, there was never a dry eye in the house. He touched everybody's emotions, because every one of us is vulnerable; every one of us is fragile; every one of us is breakable. He taught us that you can suck it in and tough it out. You can overcome. You can go through the fiery hoops, and you can make life pay you on your terms.

The world is filled with opportunities. I doubt that your problems are nearly as severe as those I've described. By taking extreme examples, I hope to demonstrate that even in the worst possible situation, those who dare can achieve amazing results. In these examples, each person touched bottom, but they bounced back. These people sank to the worst that could possibly happen to them in terms of finance, physical attractiveness, multiple losses, or ill health, but in each case, they chose to take a stand and let the setback become a step forward and a stepping stone.

Somewhere deep within them, these people found the courage to come back and triumph again.

I'm not wishing problems on you or me or anyone else. I'm saying that every problem contains within it the seed of an opportunity of an equivalent or greater benefit.

In 1922, at the young age of twenty, W. Clement Stone, whom I mentioned earlier, built an insurance agency called the Combined Registry. Later it grew into the Combined Insurance Company of America. During the Depression, while everyone else was firing salespeople, he was offering commission-only jobs, which could potentially pay as much as $10,000 a year, equivalent to $100,000 today. He hired, trained, and recruited thousands and thousands. While others were firing, he was hiring. By the time he died in 2002, at the age of one hundred, Stone owned one of the biggest and most profitable insurance companies in America.

Can you personally overcome the same kinds of obstacles? You can. If you have problems, as surely you must, can you see them as opportunities? Can you break through rather than break down? Can you break through your fear and doubt and indecision and choose to become fearless, courageous, and decisive? Of course you can.

Perhaps you're saying to yourself, "You've written about superachievers, but I'm not like that. I'm just an ordinary person without any great courage. I don't have a drive or the spiritual resources to get past my immediate problems and win great victories."

Ordinary people become extraordinary when they get pinched, pushed, or stabbed and are forced to overcome. Instead of going over all the reasons you can't do something, go for the one big reason that you *can* do it. Make a list of *why* and *how* you can, and you'll be amazed at *what* you can. You really have nothing to lose but fear of trying, and as you try, you're going to overcome. Why not go for it?

In the Bible, all the heroes have only one commonality: each and every one overcame an insurmountable problem. Each problem seemed impossible, but remember, with God all things are possible. My simple advice is pray to ask for supernatural help. God is instantly and constantly available, everywhere, always, whether you have been a believer or not. His answering service is never busy or on hold. His is a direct connection.

Let me conclude with one story. It was given to me by my friend, the extraordinary speaker and motivational coach Bob Proctor (whom you must see on You-

Tube), and it's called the 333 Story. He lives in Toronto, Canada.

In 1985, one night after the worst tornado ever in Canada, in a city near Toronto—it's called Barrie—all the mobile homes were turned upside down. There was tens of millions of dollars' worth of damage. As Bob drove through all this disaster and travail, he pulled over the car and asked himself, "Is there anything I can do about this?"

The next day he was training the sales staff at a radio station, and the owner of the radio station, Bob Templeton, had seen the same exact thing. Bob Proctor inspired Bob Templeton to ask his executives, "How would you like to raise $3 million three days from now, in just three hours, and give the money to the people in Barrie?"

Bob Templeton went up to a board, wrote the numbers "333" on it, and drew a big T below it, stretching its middle line all the way down to the bottom of the board. On one side he wrote, "How We Can." On the other side he wrote, "Why We Can't." He then drew a big X across the "Why We Can't" column and said, "Now there is no place to record the ideas we think of which explain why we can't raise $3 million in three hours, three days from now, regardless of how valid they might be."

In the end, they decided to do a radiothon and inspired fifty radio stations all across Canada to actively participate. Two of the biggest names in Canadian broadcasting agreed to host it, and three days later, they raised $3 million in the space of three hours.

You've got to ask yourself, "How can I do it?" not "Why can't I?" Because as Henry Ford said, "Whether you think you can, or whether you think you can't, you're right."

I'm saying that you can live your dreams.

FIVE

The Fundamental Secrets of Prosperity

We're talking about the fundamental secrets of prosperity. We're talking about being prosperous in our thinking, being, and living. We're going to talk about all the ways that that's going to be outpictured in our experience today.

First of all, let's talk about material prosperity, which means that you have more than enough money to pay all your bills, invest in something to make more money for you than you can spend or circulate, and still have plenty of money left over to do whatever you want, go where you want, live as you want, buy anything you want, enjoy unlimited riches, and even have surplus for philanthropy and spiritual charity.

Prosperity is much more than mere materiality. It is having close and trusting relationships with terrific friends. It's having people in your life with whom you enjoy sharing all your experiences. It means having a successful family life and living in harmony with the people you love and who love you. It means having a healthy body that is strong, vibrant, and full of energy while having peace of mind, which allows you to sleep well and contentedly each and every night. It means keeping an open and active mind, a mind that's learning and expanding every minute of every day. It means that all good things will come back to you multiplied, and your life will be overflowing with joy, friendship, love, laughter, success, health, and money.

Prosperity is that thriving state of well-being in a total sense—physically, mentally, spiritually, socially, and financially. It provides you with the freedom to do what you want when you want to do it because you want to do it. Prosperity thinking eventually fosters the true understanding that all the wealth in the universe is at your command to control, accumulate, and use. You can ultimately satisfy your every want, need, and desire.

To prosper greatly, you must be a professional thinker who knows how to control your own thinking and exclusively ingest prosperity thoughts while excluding anything that's against prosperity. We have discussed at length how the mind works. We know that we can create our own destinies in our minds. It is our mind that we must discipline to dwell exclusively on expanding our prosperity. As we've seen, whatever you think about expands. Life wants you to live fully and abundantly.

Twelve Principles of Prosperity

1. Prosperity is a state of mind.
2. Thoughts of prosperity always precede the demonstration and manifestation of prosperity.
3. My prosperity makes everyone better off and no one worse off.
4. All prosperity starts in my mind.
5. Setting prosperity goals is a necessary prelude to becoming prosperous.
6. Find a want and fill it.
7. My enjoyment of prosperity increases my prosperity.
8. I see, feel, believe, and take action toward my evolving prosperity.
9. I think big, and I achieve big results.
10. Everyone is an entrepreneur. (Many are in hiding as employees, spouses, or students.) An entrepreneur finds a problem and fixes it for a vast profit.
11. My gift of giving is a gift of receiving.

12. I have to do my own prosperity work. Nobody
    else can do it for me. Success, prosperity,
    and abundance start in your mind, get into
    your activities through the law of attraction,
    spontaneously gather a dream team, and
    generate profitable results.

Prosperity Is a State of Mind

Let's talk about the twelve principles of prosperity. First, *prosperity is a state of mind.* When I think prosperous thoughts, I become ever more prosperous, whereas thinking poor will make and keep me poor. Remember, your state of mind gives you your state of results, so you've got to think right before you can do right and receive unlimited prosperity. Most individuals would be astounded to know how many of their beliefs are attached to thoughts of lack, limitation, shortage, and have-notness.

Thoughts always reproduce themselves in our experiences. The law of cause and effect, which generates total results, is forever operative. You are as prosperous or as poor as you are right now because your life demonstrates your historical and current beliefs about yourself. Change your beliefs and ultimately you change your experience. People who think $10 thoughts get $10 results; people who think $100 thoughts get

$100 results. Earn $1 net by serving each of one billion people, and you have generated $1 billion.

People like Bill Gates, Warren Buffett, Sarah Blakely, Ted Turner, Mary Kay Ash of Mary Kay Cosmetics, and other big wealth builders started small and grew big fast. They kept expanding the prosperity horizons for themselves, their companies, their families, and their staff. With their examples, each inspired the world.

Make it a goal to read one biography or autobiography of a giant wealth builder per week, and you'll condition your mind to solve every problem profitably, as the people named above have done. I have personally read over five thousand biographies and autobiographies so far. Reading deeply and coming to know these great and inspiring success stories will make you conversationally more interesting. It will also give you solutions to business problems that will help you operate from eclectic wisdom, knowing that there is always a way to prosperity.

Ultimately each person gains prosperity out of a gargantuan product, service, or idea that they have conceived and believed in and then delivered to the public. Whatever anyone else can do, you can do if you want to do it fervently and completely enough. Your mind demands that you set the frequency dials on the amount of prosperity that you desire, deserve, and feel worthy of. The only limits are those that you self-impose.

Ask yourself: how much do I want to earn per year: $100,000, $1 million, or more? Do I want a net worth of $1 million, $100 million, or $1 billion during my lifetime? Write down your answer on a three-by-five card that says, for example: "I am so happy and glad to earn $100,000 plus a year and create a net worth of over $1 million and growing." Sign it, and get your sweetheart or business partner to cosign it and keep you accountable as you read it at breakfast, lunch, and dinner, and most importantly, just before sleep.

In India, parents inadvertently pass on poverty from generation to generation, much as in this country there are third- and fourth-generation people on welfare. The people grow up in welfare, and they think that that's what they deserve and desire, so they just keep outpicturing that. Therefore poverty begets more impoverishment. What's truly impoverished is the individual self-concept—how they see themselves, affirm themselves, and feel about themselves. Poverty is a disease of the mind. Each individual has to take the initiative to act in order to overcome poverty and become and stay rich.

The wonderful truth is that you can modify and rectify your self-concept by personal choice, instantly and constantly, and thereby create a new and better you through which to express your full self.

Thoughts of Prosperity

Principle number two: *thoughts of prosperity always precede the demonstration and manifestation of prosperity.* The ancient wisdom is, judge not by appearances, but by the right use of your good thinking. What's visibly happening on the outside world may be of little importance compared to the thoughts the individual is thinking. Your inner knower knows how to make you as prosperous as you could ever want to be, if you just dwell on the thoughts of prosperity.

The deal with prosperity is to start where you are. Aim high while forever thinking and working toward your goal. Bloom where you're planted. Whatever you want wants you more than you want it. The law of mind is that you can do as well as anyone else has ever done.

Everyone Is Better Off

Principle number three: *my prosperity makes everyone better off and no one worse off.* At the front end, if you're just going out of your way to put others in the universe in your debt, you can't know how it's going to pay off, but it will inundate you with good. You'll have a tidal wave of good coming your way.

Your prosperity needs to be all-beneficial. Why not decide to make everybody better off? "I just want to get rich for me." That's not good enough. Why not get rich for everyone, so that if anyone gets in your energy orbit, they can gain in prosperity and growth and development?

We know that we can create businesses and relationships in which everybody wins and no one loses. We're in the first time in human history when that's true. Up until now, we've been working with a competitive model, whereby somebody wins 100 percent while somebody else loses 100 percent. For the first time now in history, we have a cooperative model.

My teacher Buckminster Fuller really hit me with this principle. It's the mountain climber concept: everyone's on the same guide rope, and everyone makes it to the top. If somebody slips, everybody else pulls and works to get them back up the mountain.

That's what we're talking about here—the evolution of employee-oriented corporations. A lot of companies have ESOPs: employee stock ownership programs. UPS has a deal whereby every one of their employees can graduate from janitor to millionaire, just because they have been faithful, studied, worked, and helped out. Even truck drivers who stay for forty years plus are promised that they will retire stock millionaires, and potentially multimillionaires.

World service businesses, directed totally toward conscious and responsible entrepreneurship, now exist.

That's the new model that's coming online: you're not only doing world service, but you're doing it consciously and conscientiously. Everybody in the energy envelope is feeling good and understands that consciousness, because everybody gets to grow. At Ritz-Carlton hotels, any employee can make a decision to spend up to $500 to make a client happy. At Nordstrom's, the exact same thing applies: you give personal service and take better care of the people than they have ever been taken care of. I've done a lot of teaching at Nordstrom's. One amazing story that comes out is a lady who came in with tires and said, "I bought these tires here. You guaranteed them. I want my money back." Nordstrom doesn't sell tires, but they gave her her money back anyhow.

I think it's a cute story, and it may be apocryphal, but that's the kind of consciousness that we're looking at here. You can prosper from the Golden Rule—do unto others as you would have them do unto you—and its complement: do not do unto others what you would not want done unto yourself.

Consciousness is an echo effect. Whatever you put out comes back, except that it comes back multiplied, magnified, and magnetized, so you want to be putting out, as the Beach Boys say, good vibrations on a full-time basis. If one individual can emerge from poverty, it is likely that their example will help tens, hundreds, or maybe thousands of others to do it. Why don't you be that example? Instead of giving a handout, give a hand up. You can do something that'll have benefits that keep on paying and paying and serving and serving.

I am an example of that. I exited poverty as a twenty-something and became a millionaire. My book *The One Minute Millionaire* has inspired tens of thousands to become millionaires, with more coming soon. My first line in the book dedicated to creating a million new millionaires is: "There is no one right, easy, perfect and acceptable way for you to become a millionaire. There are a million ways to become a millionaire. Pick your perfect path to your wealth creation destiny! "

I have also taught and shared my Mega Book Marketing Seminars around the world. One man had lost his $4 million overleveraged real estate fortune and decided to deal with his adversity by wisely teaching everyone financial independence strategies. His name is Dave Ramsey. He paid $1000 twice to attend my three-day weekend intensive. Dave created his own brilliant seminars and mastered and positively exploited the church marketplace. He has also written books and now has his own TV and radio shows. He now earns over $100 million a year, using what I helped inspire him to do. I am happy to get the reflected glory. Life is an echo effect: therefore whatever you put out keeps coming back multiplied, magnetized, and magnified.

Prosperity Starts in the Mind

Principle number four: *all prosperity starts in my mind.* What I think about comes about. The great John D. Rockefeller started by saving 10 cents and got up to saving 50 cents. Then he started in the oil business and then created conglomerates to build what eventually became the ExxonMobil Corporation.

Your mind, like Rockefeller's, is potentially a source of unlimited and overflowing abundance. However, most individuals inaccurately believe that their good starts with somebody else: "If I just got that job, if I got that promotion, if I could move someplace else."

The trouble with going someplace else is that everywhere you go, you take yourself along. "If I were in some other time than right now, it would be a better time." Yeah, right. I happen to believe that this is, as Dickens wrote, "the best of times and the worst of times."

This can be the best of times if you adopt the attitude, affirmation, visualization, and verbalization that I've been describing. There's only one time, and it's *now.* You can start having your prosperity come to you right this instant by saying, "I'm on the inside of prosperity. Prosperity is inside of me." You metaphorically step inside the circle of prosperity. You'll start looking out with different eyes and see things you didn't see just a second ago, because your prosperity is hidden in plain sight. Changing your perception will change your results. No one else can give or take from you that which is yours, created by your right of consciousness, your right of awareness, your right of mindfulness. In the beginning was the word or the idea. Use that idea to say, "I'm creating prosperity in my experience," remembering always that the conceiver, you, is greater than your concept, the result. The conceiver is always going to be greater than the concept. Proof of that is happening daily to me now. Fans of my Chicken Soup for the Soul series say that they didn't think I could ever out write that series. I have lightning in a bottle for a second time with *ASK! The Bridge from Your Dreams to Your Destiny.*

Little thoughts get little results. Big thoughts get big results. Generally speaking, most people have unlimited, infinite good available to them. Anyone can start to think big, but start thinking big and then break it down into doable little parts to pull off your dreams by taking energized initiative to action.

Goal Setting

Principle number five: *setting prosperity goals is a necessary prelude to becoming prosperous.* Your first objective, as we've said, is to set goals that are definite, positive, specific, believable, desirable, and attainable. Isn't it curious in a world replete with abundance that anyone experiences lack? They probably do so because their parents or their environment or their teachers had lack thinking. You've got to start hanging out with people who do a lot of prosperity thinking and abundance thinking.

If you can't hang out with them physically, hang out with their books (like this one) or audios, because the simple truth is that you can have virtually anything you want, tangible or intangible, if you write it down and take the necessary sacrificing action to get it.

Research at Harvard shows only 3 percent of the people ever care enough about themselves to write down their true desires and work to fulfill them. When the researchers did an update on the people they studied twenty years later, they discovered that that 3 percent accomplished more than the other 99 percent combined.

Individuals who write down their goals are known to accomplish more than those who don't. I'm asking you to be an insider. Write down your goals. I know I'm being repetitive, but it's important to brand this on your brain. Start telling yourself, *I'm a master goal setter.* Go to a deeper voice if you have to, but tell yourself that.

Also remember that your belief in the possibility or impossibility of doing something predetermines whether or not you will succeed.

Your belief controls your world. From a scientific point of view, the Heisenberg indeterminacy principle says the observer modifies the thing they are observing. Same thing here. If you don't believe you can pull off real magic, like in the novels about action heroes James Bond or Dirk Pitt, you can't. I'm asking you to become the action hero or heroine in your own life. Be careful not to limit your visions by your current circumstances. Get inside the concept. Don't get locked down to a petty, limited, myopic point of view, because your concepts alone are the highways to your dreams and the realization of your loftiest desires.

The simple truth is that you can have it if you go for it with a little bit of gusto and make yourself part of that in-group of the 3 percent. Just decide, "I'm in the in-group of 3 percent, and I'm going to set these goals."

Find a Want and Fill It

Principle number six: *find a want and fill it*. That comes from Norman Vincent Peale, who said, "Find a need and fill it." I've changed one word, for a very simple reason: people do what they *want* to do and not what they *need* to do.

In the life insurance business, where I've been a trainer, I asked around and said, "What's the number one problem?" The number one problem is prospecting—

the ability to find a client. So I asked, "What would be the easiest client to find?"

I videotaped two insurance superstars, who made $100,000 a year working four hours or less a day, selling baby insurance, called Juvenile Life Insurance. That was the fastest-selling videotape ever in the life insurance business, because it was just one little want, but it filled the marketplace. One of those superstars, my agent, sold 458 baby policies, including insurance policies on both of my children, because I believe that insurance is one of the great financial vehicles. It's an easy sale, because almost everyone loves their newborns. Policies are inexpensive and almost instantly issued. People with babies know others with babies and are delighted to refer the salesperson, even going the extra mile to set up the appointments. I have seen my agent get together a group of new parents and sell everyone in the group.

One salesman at Allstate Insurance watched that video twenty-one times. He went out and earned $12,000 in the first week.

I found the need and want for that video. Then this salesman watched it and helped everybody else get baby insurance, so their kids would be guaranteed to go to college, to invest in their own business, and retire if they bought, say, a $250,000 policy. A kid could retire with $2.2 million at the age of sixty-five. They'd say, "Boy, my parents were really smart."

That's what I'm talking about. Look around and find some needs that are not quite so obvious.

There are three questions to ask a businessperson. First: "What's working?" They love to wax on poetically about that. Number two is the one you sell into: "What's not working?" Here you'll have to write notes faster than a speeding bullet. Then ask, "What would it take to increase your business 10 percent?" If you'll ask the chairman of the board, the president, the chief operating officer, and the heads of marketing and sales, you'll get different answers. You'll figure out how to solve their wants and fill them, because, as I said, people don't do what they need. They do what they want.

One of my fellow speakers said this to a poultry company. He had college interns call and ask questions of the entire company (with its permission) from top to bottom. Originally he charged the company $7,000 for his speech. With all these analytics, he offered to take this billion-dollar company up to $1.1 billion. They accepted his execution fee, which was an additional $250,000. (Another opportunity is a percentage called a success fee of, say, 10 percent. Ten percent of $100 million gross is $10 million. It's wonderful if the company will accept it and get the board of directors' approval.)

Additionally, my friend got permission to ask that client's competitors what was working, what was not working, and what could be 10 percent better in the company he was working for. Amazingly, the competitors told everything, which he wrote down and took back to the chairman of the board. The chairman gave him a very profitable multiyear contract.

Decades ago, when I was a student in Illinois, I saw people living in shacks with outhouses in the back, yet they had either brand-new or relatively new cars out front, and they had TV antennas. They needed indoor plumbing. They especially needed bathtubs and showers (as I could tell from their odiferousness when I got close to them), but they convinced themselves that they could have and ultimately did purchase cars and television sets (even if they were financed on credit), so they got what they wanted. Again, people buy what they want more often than what they need. During the Depression, women were reported to have bought makeup before buying food.

Most of us do what our peer group does. That's why I say to make sure who your peer group is. Be judicious about whom you spend your time with. My mother always used to say, "Son, to be a great man, associate with great men and women." Isn't that a classically good line? I'm so blessed that she gave it to us. Association with prosperous people who are also honest, ethical, and moral will encourage you to think, feel, and believe in your ability to prosper.

Write down the names of the ten or twelve people you spend the most time with, and next to each one write either "prosperous" or "unprosperous." Are they prosperous or unprosperous in their thinking, in their outreach, in their ability to generate money?

Now if they're just beginners, you can't fault them. If they've been around ten or twenty years working and they haven't started manifesting, then you've got to ask yourself some deeper questions, such as, "Has this person been about the business of studying prosperity from somebody that knew it, so that they got the candle touch?" Meaning that if my candle's lit and yours is not, light yours from mine. It takes nothing from mine, but makes the world proportionately brighter. I want everyone to read this book and use it to make the entire world radiant. For me, that will be reflected glory.

That's the game we're trying to play here. We'll fill everybody's wants and needs, because every one of us has at least four times more talent than we use. The goal is to live up to your potential, not your history. Say to yourself, "There's more in me." There's more talent in you, more resources, more genius, more ability. When we pull out our talents, we inspire others to do the same or more. Which of us, by suffering lack or self-imposed financial privation, can demonstrate his or her true talent? You must self-generate resources in abundance so you can easily and effortlessly afford to fulfill your destiny and inspire others to do the same.

The parable says that if you bury your talent, you lose it. Why bury it? The parable goes on to say if you multiply it, you will be given more to multiply.

Why not have enough? I'm in the information business, and I'm an information utility. I want to make sure I've got all the information of the highest and best forms so I can share it with you and so I can learn, grow, and keep developing. To underfinance the development of your great talent is to lose it. It's burying your talent to the detriment of yourself, your family, and everyone else who could have benefited from it.

I think we see that best in the classic film *It's a Wonderful Life*. The hero, played by James Stewart, is ready to jump off a bridge because he doesn't see how much good he had contributed to his family, friends, and clients. An angel shows him and saves his life. It is a must-watch classic movie.

The manifest talents that you have will reflect the light that you truly are. I assure you that you have multimillion-dollar talents. Recently a man sent me a video of how he was down and out. He came to my Mega Book Marketing Seminar and proceeded to earn $2 million in the next year. (You can watch the video at markvictorhansen.com.)

Your talents may be latent, dormant, or unexplored inside you, but you've got them. If you don't believe you've got them, just remember that *I* believe you've got them. Those talents are begging for you to get on the program. They're coded in your DNA and RNA, or you wouldn't be reading this right now. The world needs, wants, desires everyone to be totally, correctly, positively employed at their fullest, highest potential, moving toward their respective destinies.

When you get to heaven, you don't want St. Peter to take you to your heavenly warehouse and say: "Here are all your unused, saved, and beautiful talents, skills, abilities, and gifts that were yours for the asking." As Jesus graciously stated, "All I have is yours" (John 17:10).

Enjoyment Increases Prosperity

Principle number seven: *my enjoyment of prosperity increases my prosperity.* When you enjoy your prosperity, what do you do? You get to eat at the finest restaurants. You get to watch the finest sporting events in every arena. You get to go to the finest dances. You get to hear the finest music and the finest music may be Pavarotti, it may be Celine Dion—I don't know your taste, but I want to you to go to the next level of concert and lecture attendance. I want you to prosper so greatly that you can bring relatives, mentors, and friends with you at your expense. Travel is style, whatever that means to you; keep upgrading your style and taste. Be able to easily fund your lifelong educational pursuits.

You should totally enjoy whatever level of prosperity you're experiencing, because your enjoyment of prosperity will create more and more prosperity. The more you enjoy it, the more you'll have to enjoy, because your right brain creates prosperity. Your left brain will take care of the thinking and the logic, but your right brain has the feeling that'll attract more prosperity to you. If you only have $1 to invest in your experience, enjoy it. That dollar will encourage, excite, and entice you to create more dollars.

This principle even extends to paying your bills and taxes. If you enjoy paying them, you're going to have fewer bills and taxes to pay, and it's going to be easier to pay them off, so you can create new and bigger bills, and know that the same process will still hold true. It is counterintuitive, but it is true. Once you experience it, you will be elated and convinced, and you will tell all your friends.

But what do we usually do? We put ourselves in a mental cycle that works against ourselves. I call it *mental malpractice* or *self-sabotaging behavior*. You say, "I hate paying my bills." Wrong position, because if you hate something, you shut it off. You say, "I won't pay it." Then you're late paying, and they repossess your car, foreclose on your house, and shut off your telephone and your lights and heat. That just enervates you more.

I've know some people who suffer all the time, but they're really suffering from a poverty consciousness. They hoard their money like Ebenezer Scrooge. Scrooge's attitude works against you. It causes financial constipation. The ultimate effect is more and more lack. It also creates a money rejection complex mentally, emotionally, socially, spiritually, and of course financially. Pretty soon it'll cause you to be rejected from a lot of things you would have been invited to. People enjoy people who enjoy their prosperity, and the more you enjoy your prosperity, the more you'll have a positive, prosperity-attracting complex and like-minded friends. As a matter of fact, you ought to affirm to yourself, "I have a prosperity-attracting complex."

Seeing, Believing, and Taking Action

Principle number eight: *I see, feel, believe, and take action toward my evolving prosperity.* Visualization, verbalization, and imagination towards prosperity guarantee you that future realization. The imagination is the workshop of your mind.

Most of our mental attractions are to fears, doubts, indecision, pain, procrastination, guilt, anxiety, and other self-defeating, immobilizing behaviors which stifle prosperity. Imagine that your bills are paid off and up, and you've got surplus money. You can have that new car or that extraordinary lifestyle. It's available not only to the few, but to every one of us. If you control your imagination, you can cause your future direction to go where you want and realize every good thing that you imagine and much, much more.

Think Big

Principle number nine: *I think big, and I achieve big results.* Money is created in four ways. Number one is, you work. I want you to work hard. I also want you to work hard at figuring out how to leverage yourself in order to max out your results so that they have results that have results. A friend who owns one of the biggest franchises in the country says, "You work once to create the franchise, and then you get paid on an ongoing basis. I've got to look after it for maybe one hour a year," and he takes in multiple millions.

Number two: *others work.* That means that you're in management. You're in visionary leadership, because you want to use your mind power, not your behind power.

Number three: *you get money to work through investments.* I'll talk about that in chapter 6. That's easy. All you've got to do is start with a little, and I'll teach you what to do with it. If you'll just start saving $1 a day, it'll start to multiply and compound, and if you start young enough, it'll turn into a million dollars just over one work lifetime. Think about it: forty years of work times earning only $25,000 a year is a gross of $1 million. We want that to become a net of a million dollars and beyond. I'll discuss that later.

The fourth one, which I especially like, is ideas work. What are your ideas? In the parlance of information technology, this is called intellectual property or IP. This book you are reading is one of my many IPs. Henceforth I encourage you to have MSIs or *multiple sources of income.* If you limit yourself to one, it is called a JOB, which is an acronym for *just over broke.* I want you to have a real and useful MBA, redefined by me as a *millionaire's bank account.*

If you and I sat together, could you take me through your seven, ten, or twenty ideas for generating money? Most people say, "I had one idea, but it didn't work." That's not enough. We've already gone through Edison's example. He had to run out of ways that wouldn't work.

Let's go through these a little more, because the size of your thinking in each of these four categories will determine the size of your results.

1. *I work.* Are you rendering service of the highest quality and quantity service with a positive mental attitude

in order to obtain the highest possible rewards for your services and contributions, which will equal your compensation in business and life?

Most of us operate below our abilities. We live below our privileges. We know inside that this is true, which makes us feel guilty and feel as if we are less than we are.

The law of compensation has four parts:

- What is the need or demand for my product or service or idea?
- Am I competent to deliver it with excellence and self-determination to get results?
- Can I sell and market it or find a person, company, agent, or person who can?
- Is it scalable so I can earn a vast and continuous profit?

Why not outserve yourself, outthink yourself, outlive yourself? Get the results of one human being multiplied by seven to ten human lifetimes. That's what I'm trying to do. I'd like to pull off a hundred lifetimes in this one. It seems I'm doing a pretty good job. My intent is to live to 127 years young, with options for renewal.

2. *Others' work*. This is the management principle of getting results through other people. The oft-used acronym is OPW: *other people's work*. When you're good at

what you want to do, multiply yourself. Do it by associating with and creating with other people so as to get a percentage of earnings into perpetuity.

3. *Money works.* It's not enough to earn money. You should have money wisely invested so that it works harder than you do and beats the rates of inflation, deflation, reflation—all of which are happening now, whereby some products cost less and others cost more—and taxation. It's fun to study money in seminars, books, audios, podcasts, and discussions, in your mind, and in your experience. You create successful, profitable investments, and then you talk to other smart investors who know what they're talking about and can show you their results.

4. *Ideas work.* There's no limit on the value of an idea except in your thoughts, feelings, and beliefs about it. Ideas employed create prosperity. Hand along the information that you're learning here. As you grasp it, give it to somebody else. You could even build little classes among your staff, family, friends, and mastermind partners. It's good thing to have regular meetings with your peers. Join an association and contribute to it. You'll get much more back than you ever put in. I promise you this is true, because I've taken leadership roles in many associations, companies, and philanthropies.

Abe Lincoln said, "You can't make a weak person strong by making a strong person weak." Likewise, you've got to watch government and taxation, because you can't make a poor person rich by making a rich person poor. It doesn't work. Socialism sounds great, but there is no free lunch. Socialism is tested, tried, and terrible.

If you constructively teach and live these principles, it will release your individual or corporate prosperity. It'll be overflowing and ever-flowing, and the world is going to thank you in many and multiplied ways.

Tithing Creates Prosperity

Principle ten is, my *gifting, giving, and tithing creates ever expanding prosperity.*

Bob Allen (who coauthored the One Minute Millionaire series with me) and I were walking down the beach in Maui early one morning before we were to present at the Maui Writers Conference.

Bob, who is a colossal giver, asked me in a friendly and sincere way: "You wrote the classic book called *The Miracle of Tithing*. How does it really work?"

Suddenly I had a new and clearer answer. Tithing is like the three states of water. If you're a nongiver, it is like ice—frozen and relatively immobile. You are basically stifling, stopping, and detouring your flow of good and prosperity.

If you give less than 10 percent, you are like ambient water. You are in flow, but are not living in principle; therefore you're getting less than the full rewards that are available to you.

When you give 10 percent, suddenly the windows of heaven will open, as it says in Malachi 3:10, and you will receive such a rich reward that you'll hardly be able to receive it.

If you are new to this idea, it may be hard to believe and accept. So let me share my example. I am the world's best-selling nonfiction author, according to *The Guinness Book of Records*, for one main reason: I pushed and cajoled my publisher, coauthor Jack Canfield, and all subsequent cocontributors into tithing on each and every book that we write. It worked. The sale of over 500 million books is a phenomenon. My goal is to sell over one billion books.

Because of Covid-19 my wife, Crystal, and I are literally on multiple podcasts around the world daily. In one day, we did two in the United States, one in Canada, and one in Israel, and we chatted with ten million people in Vietnam. Everyone everywhere can order our books on Amazon.com and are in droves.

Previously we concentrated on American bookstores. As I write this, bookstores are struggling, and many are temporarily closed, yet book sales are up

30 percent—an all-time high, because individuals are sequestered in lockdown. They're listening to podcast voraciously and buying books in high volume.

Each of us needs to seek out our niche in which to grow rich. It's there awaiting your asking for it to fulfill your destiny.

Giving Is Receiving

Principle number eleven: *my gift of giving is a gift of receiving*. I reap what I sow. I sow generously, creatively, boldly, with an attitude of gratitude, and my gift returns to me multiplied.

What can you give? I've already talked about money, but there is much more to comprehensive giving. You can give friendship, advice, a helping hand, wisdom, insights, a smile, directions, encouragement, and more. Ask your best friend or most trusted colleague to help you generate 101 ways to give nonmaterially.

Why not become a megagiver? Everyone you meet secretly needs validation, support, an encouraging word, or an introduction that only you can give. Most are afraid to ask for help. Be the first-line giver and see if life doesn't conspire to open up and serve you in wondrous and exciting ways.

Do Your Own Work

Principle number twelve: *I have to do my own prosperity work.* Nobody else can do it for me. Nobody can eat for you. No one can think for you. No one can sleep for you. No one can think your prosperity thoughts for you. Some of you may say, "My husband's supposed to be creating prosperity for me," or "My wife's supposed to be generating the prosperity." Prosperity is an inside job. It starts in your mind. You have the right to grow to any level of prosperity you like based on your belief.

Prosperity, as Webster said, is a thriving state of economic well-being. That's true, and it's wonderful to have surplus prosperity. Money is something you need until you have enough to make you and yours feel totally, absolutely comfortable. You can get your kids through college, you can retire comfortably, and you've got excess to live on. It's good to grow through financial satisfaction into financial independence and break through to financial generosity of heart and soul. It's within your ability right now to mentally create that idea of prosperity. That comes from your *self-generated* desire (note the emphasis on *self-generated*). I can only light a candle. Hopefully, you'll light your candle on it and get a little self-generated prosperity going.

Your true desire will lead you to the decision to achieve ultimate in prosperity. Desire and decision, combined with persistent discipline, will give you any good thing you want. However, real prosperity is more than money. It's a state of mind, a standard of living, a standard of being. To achieve total prosperity, you'll want to be financially, mentally, physically, emotionally, socially, and spiritually well off. Why not have equity in every one of those areas? You can have total prosperity as outlined here. It will be omnibeneficent to you, your family, your friends, your business, your clients, and the world. Achievement happens through continuing use of your positive, evolving personalities, services, and products.

One individual with prosperity can have all the good he or she wants, but wouldn't it be nice to be really prosperous and decide that you're going to help one, ten, a hundred, or a billion? My goal is to help the eight billion others alive now to catch on to this possibility, which can be their reality.

As I suggested above, I did not know that a lockdown could be the breakthrough, but now Crystal and I can do podcasts to multiple millions while we're at home, instead of being on the road, speaking in convention centers, going to local media shows, signing books in the bookstores, and then rushing to the airport to repeat the process the next day.

I loved doing this when that was the way to do it. Now we are in a new reality. Each of us need to pivot, reinvent ourselves, and confidently become entrepreneurial, going in a new, better and more profitable direction. An entrepreneur discerns a problem and fixes it for a vast scalable profit. You are and entrepreneur. You can do this.

Look at my friend Dr. Muhammad Yunus, a Nobel Prize winner in one of the world's poorest countries: Bangladesh. Yunus founded a system of microcredit and finance, starting with $25 of his own money. He has helped over a hundred million women exit poverty. His Grameen Bank is now worth over $9 billion. Yunus says: "Everyone is an entrepreneur!" Watch him online, and be wowed. It shows what one person can do. That one person is YOU!

Your thoughts always create your world. We all can get rich, wealthy, and prosperous to the degree that we truly want to. The question is, how much do you really want? Look at what you currently have and then say, "What would I really like if I could have what I want?" Fearlessly dare to use these twelve prosperity principles. They'll work if you work them, and they'll help you to live your dream.

SIX

Gain Financial Freedom

You can have all you want financially and more. You can have joy and success and money in your future—much more than you've ever had in your past or have ever even contemplated.

As I've said, prosperity creates freedom. It is better to have more money than less money. It is better to accumulate it faster than slower. Money increases your options and your freedoms. It creates a new kind of freedom, which ends the slavery and drudgery of poverty. Poverty is a mental disease. You have to decide in favor of yourself in order to conquer it. How do we gain financial freedom? How do we find a source? If we want to be financially free, we must know that we have to begin somewhere, but where?

The answer is simple. It starts with the idea. You've got to be convinced that financial prosperity is available, persuade yourself to obtain it, accept it as it arrives, and feel good about it.

I'm going to talk about earning power and net worth power. Earning power basically is what we believe we are entitled to and deserve and which our self-image accepts. If we believe we are worth $50,000 a year, we'll study, listen, and research how to do it. If we believe we're worth $100,000 a year, which is $400 a day, 250 workdays, then we conquer that objective.

This is amazingly good news. If you can earn $100,000 a year, you can probably earn over $1 million a year if you put yourself in the right environment mentally and emotionally. It also entails having the right associates and the right opportunity . Environment is everything. Everything includes that right opportunity with the right team right now.

Opportunity is infinite. Opportunity is not outside you but inside you. It's how you decorate your consciousness and your awareness, because when you're thinking right, you'll talk right, act right, and get the right opportunities right here and now. It's in you, and it's available to you in the sweet here and now. Opportunity is first in your mind. Grasp the principle that you must become an opportunity seeker from the inside out rather than the outside in.

As my late friend Dr. Wayne Dyer said, "When you believe it, you will see it." You may not have been seeing it, because you may not have been believing it. Most people think when they see it, they'll believe it. It'll be too late then. Somebody else will already be profitably exploiting your idea.

Ideas are infinite. They flash into and out of your mind, so you must instantly record them on paper or on your computer. One idea can make you immensely wealthy. Isn't that what chewing gum did for William Wrigley? Wrigley got super-rich during the Depression selling penny sticks of gum.

Our idea was not for a best-selling book, but a mega-best-selling series: Chicken Soup for the Soul. It keeps opening up into new niche markets, which will be inspired to read everything else that we have written or will write. The principle is to create a product, service, personality, idea, franchise, benefit, or business—call it intellectual property—that becomes a cash cow. A cash cow generates endless positive cash flow forever.

You can do it. Opportunities are in your mind, awaiting your decision and desire to harvest and cash in on them. Seek and you will find. Write this affirmation on a three-by-five card: "I have an easy to implement million-dollar wow of an idea right now." If you affirm that you have a million-dollar idea and you carry it with you for thirty days, all of a sudden your subconscious starts looking for it. You'll be amazed. I've had secretaries, janitors, truck drivers come up to me who have all have used that idea. Read this affirmation four times a day: at breakfast, lunch, dinner, and, most importantly, before you go to sleep, for the next thirty days.

All of a sudden, your mind will start attracting new opportunities, because you'll be seeking them and finding them. You'll have brilliant ideas that you can have your dream team execute to your mutual benefaction, so that everybody is better off.

As a bonus, decide the drop-dead amount of cash you want to have when you sell your business. This is the amount of cash whereby, while you love the business, you would walk away from it and retire because you've got enough. Maybe your team will take over it through an ESOP—however that works out.

In one endeavor that I'm involved in, a partner just sold out his 50 percent interest to one of our other partners. We suspect he got $20 million—$5 million deposit and $2 million a year until he's paid off. Now in his late fifties, he plans to go to college and earn the degree that he's always yearned for, do a little bit of yoga, a little bit of philanthropy, and then perhaps start some entirely new businesses. The principle is to know what your exit is when you get in.

Right now is the time to embrace a big bowl of opportunity that's going to be bountiful and have more and more showing up in it. You are the one to have that idea. If you're reading this, I know that you're imagining a future earning power that's vast and enormous and has endless future possibilities.

America is the land of opportunity, and America is where the world's looking, but there are tons of opportunities everywhere and they're all available to everyone. There are more of us alive now than ever before. There are eight billion people alive on little Spaceship Earth. Each of us has needs, wants, and desires. You can choose one niche and become number one in it. I'd say pick a little niche and grow rich in that. It's easy if you believe it's easy; it's hard if you think it's hard. Famed motivational speaker Zig Ziglar used to say when we spoke together: "If you are hard on yourself, life is easy on you. If you are easy on yourself, life is hard on you."

I decided to become the number one speaker in the chiropractic business, although I wasn't a chiropractor, and I also became the number one speaker in the life insurance business. From those I jumped into the book business.

Choose a type of wealth building and accumulating activity that you would do for free because you love it so much. In the beginning of my speaking career, I knew that I loved it because I would have done it for free. I was born with this desire: I've got to speak. Now don't tell my clients, because I love that they love to invest so much in me.

The principle is, do what you love and money will inundate you. It will be effortless effort, and the money will chase you as a reward for your great service. Cavett Robert says, "Service is the rent we pay for the space that we occupy."

Once I had lunch with one of the world's greatest salesmen: the late, great Ben Feldman. Ben Feldman told me that the difference between earning $400 a day, 250 workdays a year, which equals $100,000, and $4,000 a day in 250 workdays, which is $1 million, is one zero.

The idea of that one zero kept me up thinking. He said, "You can do it." Likewise, I give you the torch that he passed me. You can do it.

I heard this idea first from W. Clement Stone. He said, "Say you wanted to earn $100,000, not in a year but in a month, because your child's life depends on it. I can tell you we'll do more for our children, who are vulnerable and innocent, than we'll ever do for ourselves. If you're kid's life depends on it, and you've got to earn that $100,000 in a month, I've seen businesspersons, salespersons, and entrepreneur after entrepreneur suck it in, tough it out, get strong, build biceps and triceps and muscles on their muscles. They do the impossible in a very short time, because they had to pay for their health needs, and the insurance didn't cover it. If the reason's there, if the *why* is big enough, your subconscious figures out the right *how*."

I've used applied kinesiology on hundreds of people in my audiences, live, in front of giant audiences, to see whether they could pull this off. Every time they said they could.

Wealth is always created the same way—repetition and duplication. Find out something that you can repeat, and then figure out how to duplicate it and upgrade it. We created the Chicken Soup for the Soul, and it sold repetitively. Then we wrote all the other niche books: *Chicken Soup for the Women's Soul*, for the mother's soul, the pet lover's soul, country soul; we have 257 more Chicken Soup books either out or planned. That's duplication.

I want to inspire you to think big, no matter how meager your experience is. As educator Dr. Ken McFarland said, "Big shots are little shots that keep shooting." Remember, there's more than enough for everyone. There's enough money for everyone to become a millionaire honestly, ethically, and morally. In America, we have a $7 trillion economy. A billion's a thousand millions, and a trillion's a thousand billions. Divide it any way you want. I want you to earn a gross of a million a year, and then earn a net of a million, and then earn a million net after taxes and tithes. It's available.

Napoleon Hill said, "It's that quantity of service plus the quality with a positive mental attitude that'll give you the unlimited compensation." You deserve unlimited compensation. I'm hereby giving you permission to yearn for it and then earn it, so that you can have pride of earnership and pride of ownership.

I hope at some future time to meet with you and hear your phenomenal success story, which couldn't have happened until you read this, got the idea, and then went out and realized it.

I can imagine you telling me how no one in your family had ever achieved financial freedom before you, how many people you have helped, how good it feels, and how it happened faster than you ever believed possible, and describing all the accolades, rewards, friendships, travel, philanthropy, charity, and the total excitement of being tuned in and turned on. I expect to hear from you.

Allow me to think out loud with you one more time. Someone like you decides in favor of himself or herself. You start to make a magnificent and important difference. You positively affect 250 people in ways that you'll never know. Divide 8 billion by 250: we need 32 million individuals who choose to make a difference and have a pride of earnership. We call those people difference makers, history creators, and world leading transformers, and I see that you're going to be one of them, no matter what you call yourself. You're the one, and if you share this one idea with somebody else, soon we'll discover those 32 million other difference makers. They're there, waiting to be ignited to their greatness. Given all the tools at my command and those I'll discover—TV, Internet, podcasts, books, audios, documentaries, webinar funnels, videos, seminars—how can we miss, working together? So start small.

When I was a child, I earned $1 an hour cutting lawns. Now I earn over $1 a second. It's all relative. We all start low and build as high as we choose to go if we create massive value for our customers and clients. People are hungry to have innovation, and you can do it as a person that's decided to get his or her earning power together. John Wesley, founder of the Methodist movement in the eighteenth century and said to be the richest minister alive at the time, advised, "Earn all you can, save all you can, invest all you can, and then give all you can."

Let's go on now to finances and building your net worth. With your net worth, you've got seven basic choices to play with. I'll just give an overview, and then we'll go into them specifically.

1. Banks.

2. Life insurance.

3. Stocks, bonds, and mutual funds.

4. Antiques, art, and collectibles.

5. Gold, silver, and diamonds.

6. Your own business.

7. Real estate.

Savings and Banks

There are many different kinds of banks: savings banks, credit unions, commercial banks, private banks, investment banks, and investment trust banks. But savings is the start of all wealth creation. Think of your savings account as your temporary storage account, waiting to be wisely and profitably invested for a net operating income (NOI).

You've got to be a saver. The goal here is to save 10 percent of your money, which is a wise, wonderful, and prudent decision to make. If you need to be reinforced in this, read *The Richest Man in Babylon* by George Clason. He'll sell you on savings, because savings builds your self-esteem. It's the start of all financial freedom and independence.

A savings account is usually insured by the Federal Deposit Insurance Corporation (FDIC). They tend to pay relatively low interest rates, meaning that after taxes, the amount that goes to you is considerably reduced, but remember, this is the first vehicle you use.

Bank savings accounts are now paying about 1 percent. That's why you are only storing it until you can get a higher and better ROI.

It is important that you learn the law of 72. Basically, it says if you divide the number 72 by any interest rate you earn, that will show how fast your money will doubles. At a 1 percent rate of return, it takes 72 years for $1 to become $2.

Know that credit cards based in South Dakota can charge up to 79.9 percent legally if they disclose it to the borrower. The problem is, who reads the small print or humbly asks to have it thoroughly and completely explained?

Desperate and ignorant people get absorbed into these usurious credit scams. At a 79.9 percent interest rate, your bill to the credit card company doubles every nine months. If you owed $1,000, you now owe $2,000, with interest compounding on all of it. That's why the borrower should beware. Few people know this, so many are taken advantage of because of their ignorance.

Many individuals are abused by the system of credit only because no one taught them to understand the truth about money lending, borrowing, and multiplying. Don't let that be you. I wish that in all schools all students were required to pass a class in financial awareness of this kind before graduation.

You need to decide how much you want in savings and how much you want in your emergency reserve fund, often called a rainy-day fund. Everybody's got to have an emergency reserve fund. Most financial advisors recommend three to six months' worth of earnings as a safety cushion against loss of employment, sickness, a family emergency, or a pandemic. Therefore, if you're earning $4,000 a month, your minimum three months savings reserve should be $12,000. It's ideal to have this savings in a high-earning or a higher-yielding money market account. It'll earn more for you and you'll still have financial liquidity, because you'll be able to write up to three checks a month and stay alive until you reinvent yourself and your occupation and get back on your feet again.

For this, you've got to talk to your banker, and I'll put another bonus point in here. Make sure you befriend your banker. Have their home phone number. Be on a first-name basis. Put them on your A-party list. Send them a birthday card with a personally written note every year. Follow them as they change banks or institutions. Socialize with them a little bit, because bankers can leverage you over time in a myriad of helpful ways. But remember, as you get richer, their advice may no longer suffice for your advances in status and wealth.

Life Insurance

The next investment vehicle is life insurance. As far as I'm concerned, life insurance and disability insurance are necessary for everyone. Life insurance is bought for pennies on a dollar. Ben Feldman used to lay down a $1 bill; he'd have three pennies under it and say, "I'm selling a dollar at three cents on the dollar. How many do you want?" The earlier in your life you purchase life insurance, the less it costs and the more value it has. I've got life insurance on myself and my wife. I bought life insurance for both my daughters at birth. They were guaranteed money to go to college, buy their own businesses, and if they choose to, retire with financial dignity. This is a lot of powerful guarantees, and it's a permanent kind of "gimme." Buy policies only with great and lasting insurance companies, and once you buy it, keep it. Do not let your agent roll over your policy. It benefits him or her but rarely benefits you.

Life insurance comes in three basic forms: term insurance, universal life, and whole life. I'm going to keep this simple. If you're insurable, get insured now. Term insurance is a great way to start your program when you're financially thin or just at the beginning of your wealth creation. Billion-dollar companies have emerged with a slogan, "Buy term and invest the difference." But according to multiple insurance studies, few people invest the difference they save with term insurance. Even so, term is better than no life insurance at all. The problem is, when you need it most, say, at age seventy-five, eighty-five, or ninety-five (because you're going to live long and prosper), it won't be there for you. It's sort of like bedwetting. It's a temporary expedient, but in the long term it leaves you cold. You basically put your money in the sand.

The second type is universal life insurance. It mixes the benefit of term insurance, the low cost, with tax-deferred cash buildup that'll be there when you need it most, for your family at your death. It gives you value that can't run out before you do. Our longevity is forever expanding because of break-throughs in medicine, nutrition, fitness, science, and technology. If you're going to live longer, you want to make sure you don't use up all your money until the day after you're dead. You want to have cash flow when you need it and not have it depleted until you're gone.

Many companies are now selling life insurance that goes to 120 years. Additionally, you can buy a *term rider*, which pays you back when you collect it, assuming you live to the end of your policy, with all the premiums you've invested also returned in full to you.

Whole life insurance is money that grows in a permanent, guaranteed, predictable fashion. It is solid, and it's a nontaxable asset. You can borrow money against your building asset at an incredibly low rate. Basically, you are borrowing your own money. Walt Disney did this to build Disneyland. If you can afford it, put some part of your portfolio into whole life insurance.

Estate insurance is another area that can be discussed with your life insurance agent, financial advisor, planner, estate, or tax attorney. You've got to choose a great agent and a great attorney. The right attorney is worth millions; the wrong attorney is going to cost you millions. I have been with both.

If you want the best life insurance person available, here are some qualifications and characteristics to look for. He or she should have been in business for over a decade. A recommendation leading you to that person from a wise, independently wealthy person is a superb idea. Qualifications they should have are chartered life underwriter (CLU) and certified financial planner (CFP), both of which are professional designations they have to earn. Preferably they're members of the life insurance industry's Million Dollar Round Table, another honor that they earn. If they are superstars, they are invited into what is called Top of the Table.

Additionally, if you can afford it, get disability insurance. Your chances of getting disabled during your career is six times greater than your chance of death. Today disability insurance is difficult to secure because of tough times. Many policy holders have had to take advantage of it, and they've overtaxed the reserves of our great financial institutions. Usually you can obtain insurance that will pay 60 percent to 90 percent of your income if you are disabled. It's expensive, but not nearly as expensive as not having it when you need it.

Another little-known secret is that with some policies you can get *living death benefits* (LDB.) If you get sick or disabled while insured, these policies can pay off your healthcare expenses while you are alive. You can pay back your premiums when you are back on your feet again and be insured again in full, so it is a double win.

A friend of mine who's a highly credentialed financial planner asks his clients, most of whom are medical doctors, "If you were a doctor, would you prefer to work for a hospital that pays you $100,000 a year and if, God forbid, you became permanently disabled and could not practice, you would earn nothing, or would you rather work for $97,000 a year, and if you became disabled, you would earn $55,000 a year tax-free for life?" My friend finds that 100 percent of the time, they choose the latter scenario. He says, "They just write a check to my insurance company." It's a very simple thing. Everybody needs disability if they can afford it.

Stocks, Bonds, and Mutual Funds

I can only give you a brief overview here. As I write this, the stock market is setting extravagant new records, with no immediate end in sight. Remember, after every boom there is a bust. Wise investments in good stocks always pay off at about 10 percent in the long term. The world's greatest and richest investor, Warren Buffett, who has all his money in the stock market, believes that the minimum length of an investment is forever.

Please truly note that Buffett is not a stock investor so much as a company buyer. He buys most of the company, rather like a hedge fund, and then vertically integrates the companies he owns so that each does business with and buys from the others.

Buffett started with $100 and created the equivalent of a mutual fund called Berkshire Hathaway. At the end of 2019, he was worth $80.8 billion personally. He learned value investing from the great Ben Graham. He buys stocks in companies whose value is greater than their price, meaning that if they had to sell out and liquidate instantly, he'd still make a profit. His comments are always witty, wise, and succinct. Almost everybody in investments reads his annual reports. I encourage you to read, study, and understand the work on or about him.

I predict that the next Warren Buffett will be my friend Bill Staton, known as "America's Money Coach." Bill wrote a must-read book called *America's Finest Companies*. From his extensive research, Bill discovered that America's finest companies have had ten continuous years of increases in earnings and dividends. He recommends that you invest in ten different industries—for example, electronics, pharmaceuticals, real estate, retail—from his list of America's finest companies, the proven superstars. It's possible one of these sectors could experience a financial hiccup, but it's unlikely that ten out of then will. Therefore you're covered and you've made yourself a mini-mutual fund.

Bill audaciously said, "If at a young age—say at twenty-five years old, you start investing pocket change, $50 a month, in ten or more of these companies once a year, you will retire a millionaire way before you turn sixty-five."

I tested the theory on my daughters, Elizabeth and Melanie, at one time when they were ten and eight years old. I gave them Bill's list. I said, "Here's a highlighter. Highlight the ones you want."

It's amazing that the girls picked stocks in companies they knew, and they made brilliant choices. If little kids can pick out good companies that they see are going to make it—like Hershey and McDonald's and General Electric and Intel and Microsoft—I think anyone can do it.

The next category is bonds. This is unequivocally the most conservative way to go. The expert advisor I listen to here is a guy who's made 28,000 doctors multimillionaires. His name is Greg Stanley. He's CEO of Whitehall Management and recommends AAA municipal bonds in certain areas. He says, "You've got to have a broker that really knows this area."

Bonds are the safest and the most risk-averse investment plan in America. The bad news is that they require a minimum investment of $5,000 at a time. Who plays this game? Ross Perot used to wake up every January 2 with $200 million double tax-free: that means no state and no federal tax. That would give you a way to circulate money during the year and not have to worry about it.

The next category is mutual funds. Mutual funds are a way of investing in multiple stock offerings through a company that picks them. There are load and no-load funds. You're going to have to study this a little bit, but many people in America are pretty savvy about mutual funds. You want to a mutual-fund company that's got longevity and a really good track record.

Art, Antiques, and Collectibles

Next is a fun one: art, antiques, and collectibles. Art is an appreciating asset, as are antiques and collectibles, especially if you buy famous or soon-to-die artists. Here too you need to have an art dealer, a broker, or an estate salesperson. If you start going to some estate sales and you get savvy, you can make money in everything. I have a friend who's made multiple millions. He's an Iranian gentleman who buys Persian carpets, and he knows what he's doing.

You want to get really good things. As your wealth expands, like most people, you'll be naturally inclined to go to museums, art galleries, and shows. Antiques shows, though, are unique. Most investors start by choosing a period like Early American, Louis XIV, or the Roman period. Billionaire John Paul Getty was a scholar in Greek and Roman art, and his collection is lavishly on display at his home on the Pacific Coast Highway and at his $4 billion museum, both of which are in Los Angeles.

As you study these collections and visit antiques stores, you'll be amazed how much is available, how good the antiques are, and how well they appreciate. Most faithfully appreciate 10 percent or more a year. If you study these great collections, of John Paul Getty, of Liberace in Las Vegas, the John Deere Museum in

Florida, the Hearst Mansion in San Simeon, California, Andrew Carnegie's home, (now a museum run by the Smithsonian Institute at Fifth Avenue and 95th Street in New York), you'll start to understand the asset value of antiques and collectibles. As you travel, decide to go to every rich person's home or museum that's open to the public.

Include in those visits presidential museums around the country, such as Teddy Roosevelt's on Long Island; Franklin Roosevelt's in Hyde Park, New York; Reagan's in Simi Valley, California; Nixon's in Yorba Linda, California; and Harry Truman's in both Key West, Florida, and in Independence, Missouri. Plan almost a day at each. Take pictures, make notes, and bring your kids or grandkids. It will be an unforgettable lifelong memory and a way to truly feel and reexperience American history.

Collectibles can include anything from cars and watches to dolls to toys to baseball cards. The specialty I mastered is autographs. I have collected autographs for four decades, and I have a collection worth $2 million. Famous autographs just keep appreciating. A lot of them were from people I thought would still be around, yet they've light-beamed off the planet.

You may be saying, "There's no way I can do that." Let me give one example: an autograph collector I met in Cleveland. He happens to be a certified public accountant. Every morning before he goes out to work, he spends two hours out in front of the Ritz-Carlton. He sees who is being escorted out, and he asks, "Can I have your autograph?" I gave him three different autographs myself in different places. He's got $200 million worth of autographs, all from standing outside of one Ritz-Carlton and merely asking every famous person exiting or entering the hotel for their signatures. I assume he befriended the doorman or concierge in order to get the inside info on who was at the hotel.

You may tell me, "I can't get rich." This guy didn't pay one cent for these autographs, but he sells them. I saw him go up to each celebrity and get their autographs. All of them, like author Sidney Sheldon, were pleased to do it. This is an easy moneymaking technique.

Gold, Silver, and Diamonds

The next one is gold, silver, and diamonds. Wealth teachers advise that you have in safe keeping, perhaps in a bank safety deposit box, ten percent of your wealth in the above items. Diamonds are the lightest and most transportable in an emergency. Junk silver is usually sold by the bag and valued based on the coin, weight, and wear of the product. If there were to be a depression, you'd be well advised to have a bag full of junk silver dimes and quarters. In such times, currency tends to vary wildly in value, as in Argentina today or back in Germany's Weimar Republic after World War I, where people carried cash in wheelbarrows to buy a loaf of bread.

Gold is usually in the form of coins, like American Eagles, South African Krugerrands, or Canadian Maple Leafs, although it sometimes comes in the form of bullion pieces, which are a heavy to carry around or even to keep in your safe or safety deposit box. Safety is obviously a key factor here.

If you're a beginner, I would not recommend gold certificates or any gold paper. These assets have a way of not being there when you need them the most. But actual gold in your possession is a wise buy and hold.

I believe that you ought to have some gold, silver, and diamonds. Wear them so you feel prosperous and so get to be more prosperous. Currently it is not safe to flash your wealth, so only wear valuable jewelry at home or when you are entirely safe or in surroundings you know. Do not take it on international trips.

Your Own Business

Next is one that I'm really keen on: owning your own business. Be an entrepreneur. Be a risk taker. Find some business that's exciting, that really juices you, that you want to go into every day and really have pride of ownership in.

Owning a business may be one of your lifelong goals. If it is, I suggest you carefully choose a business that is based on your heart's desire. First, study it intensively. Then join the industry association. Interview at least ten to twenty men and women in that business before you enter it and ask every possible question. Before launching Chicken Soup series I interviewed 101 best-selling fiction and nonfiction authors. I thought I knew how to write effectively. I asked, how did you market so many books? I got over 202 extraordinary answers that I compiled into a wow of a business plan, and still 144 publishers rejected it. So take copious notes.

You will be amazed to find that a lot of them are willing to sell their businesses. Many would even give them to you without charging you any cash if you agree to be your own broker. Use your intuition to discover what to ask for; maybe whisper, "Is your business for sale?" Almost every business is for sale for the right price.

Think it through anew. Go to some business opportunity meetings. Go to some financial expos and association meetings. One guy that hired me long ago had a franchise owners' association meeting. He charged everyone from McDonald's to Marriott to attend. The audience listened to me and many other phenomenal presenters and absorbed every detail over three intense days.

I said this above, but it bears repeating. Ask everybody what works, what doesn't work, and what would cause a 10 percent increase in profit. Interview both the best and the worst in the business, and find out what works and doesn't work.

Decide if you want to apprentice yourself to somebody. History teaches that every great was an apprentice for two years or more to some other great. Be innovative. Be creative. Be resourceful. History teaches that every great individual was an apprentice for two years or more to some other great. I studied with Dr. R. Buckminster Fuller as a research assistant for most of seven years, and the effect was life improving to the max. Look for that niche to grow rich in that could be uniquely yours.

Real Estate

The last category for building your net worth is real estate: 90 percent of the millionaires in the world own real estate. Now that's true even in Bill Gates's case, although he owns the real estate that Microsoft is in. McDonald's real asset is that they own all the land that all their restaurants occupy worldwide, so when they sell a franchise, they know they've got an anchor client that can't miss. You could do the same thing. Just like the stock market, real estate appreciates year in year out at about 10 percent, except when it has a hiccup, as it did after the Great Recession.

The game is buy low, sell high. The principle is that you make your money on the buy. My friend Bob Allen teaches lots of ways to do this in his book *No Money Down*, but real estate is a psychological market more than a hard cash market. If you look around, you can always find a good deal. I play around in it both residentially and commercially. We buy yucks that make big bucks. We buy the worst houses in the best neighborhoods—the fixer-uppers—bring them up to standard, and either rent them out or sell them.

You can do both. My first single-family residential investment cost me $14,000 with a $2,000 deposit in 1974 in East Islip, Long Island, New York. From the get-go, it had positive cash flow; it paid for itself. I sold it ten years later for a $58,000 net profit. I should have bought all the fixer-uppers in East Islip, but I didn't; I missed that season. It made me pay attention, because we are entering another, bigger season thanks to the coronavirus. "To every thing there is a season, and a time to every purpose under heaven" (Ecclesiastes 3:1).

Real estate is extraordinarily profitable if you do your homework before you do your investing. There are a million ways to make a million in real estate (and probably a million ways to lose it too).

I want to recommend several books in this field. One is Bob Allen's *No Money Down*. The others are Ken McElroy's books on real estate; he is a wise friend who owns over ten thousand units and daily goes on YouTube sharing his brilliance and immediate experiences. Both are great people, whom I know intimately. Both are investors, and that's why I recommend their works.

Note the principles of supply and demand, such as migration patterns, which can be seen by watching U-Haul movements and checking where lots of new driver's licenses are being issued. As I write this, there is a vast egress out of New York City and an ingress into Florida, Arizona, and Texas. Because so many are unemployed, real estate prices are expected to decline, and rentals are expected to vastly increase.

As for commercial real estate, I'm going to recommend a work by another friend, who is the world's biggest commercial investor. He's a lovely guy, named Trammell Crow, down in Dallas. He is a man of integrity, generosity, and wisdom. His sons, Harlen and Trammel Jr., and his sister, Lucy, now run the company. If you read Trammel Crow's autobiography, *Master Builder*, it'll tip you off to a lot of commercial real estate wisdom.

*   *   *

If you think through these seven network positions and balance your portfolio, you can live your dreams and live off the money made by your money—and again, congratulations in advance!

SEVEN

Create a Dream Team

want to make your dreams come true. I want to make you supersuccessful, and the easy, effortless way to do that is for you to create a dream team. I'm going to tell you how to do it, and the results are going to be extraordinary. You're going to become enormously successful and help a lot of other people. It makes all the difference to you, your future, and tens, hundreds, maybe thousands, millions, even billions of other people. If you'll just get into a team, you'll get to realize your dream.

TEAM is an acronym that means *Together Everyone Achieves More* (or *Together Everyone Achieves Miracles)*. As far as I'm concerned, participating in a dream team is one of the most critical elements in living your dream.

It is the one way to get support and supply your dreams with an unlimited source of energy so that they get business and life.

A dream team alliance is two or more individuals that voluntarily come together to creatively put their energy behind one definite major purpose. When I'm teaching this at a seminar, I tell people, "Extend your two index fingers, and put them together. You'll see that one and one equal eleven. That's what a dream team is."

When you've gotten your dream team together, you can create miracles. Those miracles work for solving problems in business as well as in the family, because together we accomplish more when we're unified, when we're allied, when we're shoulder to shoulder and back to back.

A team is like a flashlight. A flashlight always requires two batteries; if you've only got one, it's powerless. They've got to be harmonically placed, then you press the button and voilà! The flashlight lights.

Miracles can only happen when two or more are gathered together and operating in perfect harmony. You can only bring out your full talents, your full resources, and your full abilities when you have a resource team that's strong where you're weak. Other people trigger us. They stimulate us and motivate us to become all we're capable of being. As part of the dream team, you use blended mind power and action to obtain your desired result. None of us can be totally successful alone. We need other people to energize our outlook and find the best that's in us and in the group. Each of us needs all of us, and all of us need one another. We need others to see more in us than we see in ourselves. We need others to support, encourage, and empower us and to enhance our relationship with one another and with our greater purposes.

When two lit candles are brought together, an amazing thing happens: the flame jumps fourfold. Whole systems are the behavior of the sum of the parts. A dream team works that way: it gets stronger and stronger.

The ancient wisdom says that one person can move a thousand, but two can move ten thousand (Deuteronomy 32:30). It's like the great Clydesdale horses. One can pull a small amount of weight, but two can pull far more. When you get six of them in tandem, they can pull almost anything. These synergies and serendipities will wow you. Together we can hold the space of possibility that one person could never hold alone.

When Jack and I started our dream team to build the Chicken Soup for the Soul phenomenon, once in a while he'd oscillate and say, "I don't know if this is going to be the best book ever or the worst and if it's going to go downhill." I held the vision for him. Likewise, he had to hold the vision for me, because no one can be strong all the time, but together two can be strong. When you get a cut on your hand, the skin grows back stronger than it's ever been.

When you have your dream team, you wake up creativity. You wake up intuitive powers. You get this synergetic new mind. No one mind is ever complete. When you're really on task about a project, you find yourself waking up in the middle of the night; the next day you talk to the other person. If you're both on task, you catch the illumination at the same time. It's amazing.

When you get a real team together, you get your dream together. When Bill Gates was running Microsoft, his dream team had more points of IQ than any company in history. They called themselves "propeller-heads," and he said, "We have breakthrough after breakthrough after breakthrough." He's succeeded because he's brought out the best and the brightest.

Individuals harmonically working together with a purpose are unstoppable, and they always make a profound difference. It's the vital essence of a dream team: friendly individuals working in total synchronization to achieve a purpose or purposes bigger than themselves. They all outperform themselves. They outserve themselves. They outwork themselves. They do real magic because they have real magic to do. The old cliché is, "United we stand, divided we fall." We need to have a place where we can go to be shoulder to shoulder with somebody, and back to back when you're getting attacked.

To become a great person, a great entrepreneur, parent, leader, speaker, author, spouse, teacher, scientist, politician, thinker, or athlete, you've got to have a dream team. In this relationship, one person may be invisible, with only one out in front, but a team is the prerequisite of greatness, I promise you. Note the motto on the Great Seal of the United States: *e pluribus unum*: out of many, one.

Read any biography or autobiography, and you will find the dream team relationship. I challenge you to read at least a hundred biographies and autobiographies: that would be a good beginning. It will inspire you. It will give you concepts and tools that you can use for the rest of your life. I have read biographies and autobiographies of everyone from Bill Gates to Walt Disney, from Aristotle Onassis to the Wright brothers, from JFK, who always had the best and brightest minds, to Winston Churchill. Time and again, you'll find that greatness depends on two or more individuals working together.

I used to be on the board of the world's biggest privately held airline, Evergreen Airlines International, headquartered in McMinnville, Oregon. We had a board of directors that was a dream team alliance with twenty-eight people. We had a four-star general, a former head of the Military Air Command (MAC). We had the former head of YUZ aircraft. One time when he came, he brought original tintype videos of Orville and Wilbur Wright.

At one point Orville and Wilbur were in the hospital together. Their bodies had both been crushed by failure after failure in creating an airplane. Orville said to Wilbur, "You know, maybe that Frenchman's coefficient of lift and drag is wrong." Lying in the hospital together, recuperating for six weeks, they recalculated it, and it was off by just one degree. It's the little difference that has a big effect. When I'm on a flight that's taking off, the airplane just goes up one degree, but after a short time, it's seven miles into the air, and it goes into straight into level flight. In aviation, it's called the trim tab effect, whereby the littlest tip of the trailing edge of the wing takes the plane into high flight.

The same principle applies here. Two individuals get together; they have the power of eleven. It won't wear out, rust out, tire out, or go on vacation. It works for each of us who employs it. It raises us to new standards and new possibilities of excitement, and it levels out as it expands.

I challenge you to create one dream team, and what'll happen is you'll have another and another. Your capacity to be and do and have will geometrically increase, and you'll become a better individual. Your association with like-minded individuals will make you more well-rounded. You'll think about things that are beautiful, lovely, noble, and of good report, and you'll figure out how to be a real world server. The possibilities are endless.

Dream teaming always start with an idea in one person's mind communicated in an omnieffective way to another person's mind.

Basically, the relationship is like a marriage. Two people get mentally married, and then they decide what's going to come of it. When each person gives 100 percent of his or her energy, the amount of available energy doesn't multiply to 200 percent, but it magically goes to 400 percent, 500 percent, 1000 percent, and you get much more out of the relationship than you expect.

When Bill Gates was a beginning student at Harvard University, the computer was just coming online. Gates got together with Paul Allen, who was a couple of years older, and they said, "Holy cow. This computer thing is really going to work," so Bill dropped out of Harvard. They went down to New Mexico to start their first computer company and came up with the name Microsoft. They went up to Bellevue, Washington, and the rest is history. Microsoft was one of the fastest-growing companies ever, just because two guys had the gumption to drop out of school and do something that had never been done before.

The question is, "How do I start my group? I don't know anyone of influence." You become a person of influence by getting yourself on a dream team. Decide on the abstract. Decide conceptually. Make it an idea that you're that person of influence and you're going to enroll another person, a friendly, like-minded individual. Decide that the two of you are going to meet regularly. Then add selected members unanimously agreed upon by both of you.

My friend Dan Sullivan suggests asking potential members this question: "If we were to get together three years from today, what would have had to happen to make you feel happy, successful, and fulfilled?" If they won't share this with you, they don't trust you. Do not consider them as potential wayfarers who will give you a bigger, brighter, greater, grander future. Pick your dream team members because they have big potential futures that include you and that they want you to be part of, and you too want to be part of their lives.

Each new member has to be put on probation, because you don't know whether somebody belongs on your dream team until there's a mishap—there's a major problem, somebody's suing you, things go wrong. Everyone loves you when you're in high flight. When you start to get dented and kicked around, you'll find out who gets to stay and who doesn't. During good times, it's hard to see when synergy works and when it doesn't. When the yogurt hits the fan, you need people that'll stand strong.

The idea of having a support group precedes its creation and integration, the support you'll get out of it, and the phenomenal outpouring of results, expected and unexpected. Choose to form your group carefully. Write down in the abstract where you're strong and where you're weak. Pick people that are strong where you're weak. Attract into your group the best and the brightest, the most cooperative minds available, individuals who want to be on purpose for themselves and others. To repeat, admit new members only by unanimous consent and after putting them on a three-month probation.

Also, do an online search for the individual's name and the keywords *fraud, criminal record, bankruptcies, credit defaults,* and so on. You want to know their faults before you let them in your group. This has been a hard-learned and superexpensive lesson for me.

Dale Carnegie taught that the most critical thing for each member to bring to the meeting is a positive mental attitude. If you've got people that are negative, selfish, critical, or demanding, they'll destroy your group, so kick them out early.

As for meetings, choose to meet at least weekly for an hour to an hour and a half. When I was building my speaking business from the front end, real estate salesman Chip Collins and I met, and it was almost like a religious experience for both of us. By the end we were so buoyant that we were unstoppable. If I went in to present at one of his sales meetings, they almost bought before I got in the room, because I was pumped; I was psyched.

The meeting has got to be a life-enhancing priority. If it's really going to be a true dream team, everybody has got to be upbeat, enriched, encouraged. They're going to benefit each other. You ask what's going right, and you also ask what's going wrong. Usually if somebody has something going wrong, somebody else in the group knows how to set it right again.

It's nice to start with some positive, uplifting story. Use one of my books or *Think and Grow Rich*. Or ask, what's the best thing that happened to you this week? Or start with humor and jokes. We learn from neuro-linguistic programming that laughter gets us to breathe together and to resonate heart to heart, soul to soul.

Each individual must demonstrate their abilities, resources, and talents to contribute generally to the good of the group and each other for a purpose bigger than themselves. The contribution may be contacts, money, support, goodwill, education, experience, resources, ideas, strategies, or talent. They've got to give energy to the group; they can't come and suck it off.

Let me share the guidelines for creating your dream team in action.

1. The average group works best with two to six members, preferably no more than twelve. (Even though I said that that airline board had more, those were all superstar professionals.)

2. Meet regularly, weekly if possible. Meet in a nice, preferably inspirational place if possible. It could be a diner. It could be your office. It could be at home. It could be at a church. It could be at a library. It could be anyplace that's comfortable without too much interruption.

3. Start the meetings by reading the following principles. I wrote these principles for you, and I think you're going to like them:

I release. I release myself to the group, because I'm stronger when I have the help of others.

I believe. I believe the combined intelligence of the group creates a wisdom far beyond my own.

I understand. I will more easily create positive results in my life when I am open to looking at myself and my problems from another's point of view.

I decide. I decide to release my desires totally and to trust in the group, and I am open to accepting new possibilities.

I forgive. I forgive myself for the mistakes I have made. I also forgive others who have hurt me in the past so I can move into the future with a clean slate.

I ask. I ask the group to hear what I really want—my goals, my dreams, my desires, my destiny—and I hear my partners supporting me in my fulfillment.

I accept. I know, relax, and accept, believing that the working part of the group will respond to my every need. I am grateful knowing this is so.

Dedication and covenant: *I now have a covenant in which it is agreed that this group shall supply me with an abundance with all things necessary to live a success-filled and happy life. I dedicate myself to be of maximum service to God and my fellow human beings, to live in a manner which will set the highest example for others to follow, and to remain an open channel. I go forth in the spirit of enthusiasm, excitement, and expectancy.*

4. Have each member share something positive that has happened to them since the last meeting, or have each person say something sincere, genuine, and self-esteem building about the other dream team partners.

5. I have each member share the problem or opportunity that they have experienced since the last meeting, and the support that they would like to get in solving it.

6. The member should be supported visually, verbally, and feelingly by others. For example, someone wants a new home. Other members might say, "I see you driv-

ing up to your glorious new home. I see the circular driveway you've always dreamed of. I see the bedroom that's so big you're going to have to have a sit-down vacuum to clean it." Get the support out of it.

After the meeting, you're going to have an elevated sense of well-being. You're going to feel connected to a higher spiritual source. New energy is going to flow through your heart, mind, body, and soul. A salesperson like me will go into a sales meeting tuned in and turned on. You could put the toughest prospect in front of me, and I'll melt them down. I'll make my offer irresistible. Why? Because I have the full force of this group working with me.

After the meeting, secure the exact date and time for the next meeting. Make sure you give everyone permission to call one another, especially with good news, because this is a self-fulfilling prophecy. We can start to resonate or bubble up and get our dream team to grow.

Michael Jordan is unequivocally the highest-paid basketball player in history, but he wasn't always that way. The first two years he was in high school, they made him sit on the bench. They said, "You're no good. You're never going to amount to anything." He kept saying, "I'm massively innovative. I'm massively innovative." He started slam-dunking from a half-inch, then from an inch, then from midcourt, and eventually he became the highest-paid athlete of all time.

What did he say about a team? "If you want me to play, you've got to hire Phil Jackson as coach. I need Dennis Rodman to rebound. I need a champion team. These are my demands, or I won't play."

That's how you ought to feel. You want to bring out the best championship team, and you want to bring out the self-esteem and self-reliance of each member. You will then expand at a quantum level. That's how the best get better: you'll start having projects that have projects, encounters that have encounters. You'll transcend yourself.

Andrew Carnegie thought the most important principle he ever learned was to have a mastermind team. He got together with one man, Charles M. Schwab, while he was shoveling coal at 18 cents a day. He asked Schwab, "Do you want to become rich someday?" They went from being laborers earning pennies a day to creating a vision of becoming the world's biggest steel company. Ultimately Carnegie paid Schwab the outrageous bonus of $1 million a year for outperforming, outserving, outthinking, and outselling himself. Both men worked enthusiastically together, always going the extra mile personally and professionally. They created new possibilities together that neither individual alone could have imagined.

Andrew Carnegie was called the Old Scotsman. He went from rags to riches during his lifetime, becoming the world's richest man, because he apprehended, comprehended, and used this principle. Listen to what he said: "I knew little of marketing and manufacturing steel. I surrounded myself with more than a score of men and women whose combined education, experience, and abilities gave me the full benefit of all that was known. My job was to keep the men inspired to desire to do the finest job possible. I have a system of compensation which permits every member of my group to name his or her own financial reward, but the system is arranged that beyond a certain maximum salary which each person is allowed, an individual must establish definite proof that he or she earned more than that amount before they receive it. The system encourages self-initiative, imagination, enthusiasm, and leads to continuous personal growth and development."

Someone told Henry Ford that he was not an educated man. He said, "Look, I have buttons on my telephones. If I need a PhD, I'll press a button and get one."

Two guys, starting in a little garage in 1959 in Ada, Michigan, built a company that now does over $12 billion a year. Called the Amway Corporation, it directly employs over two million distributors around the world, selling in excess of two thousand products.

You can start small and become great. If you ever go to Ada, Michigan, go through the Free Enterprise Center there and see the American art and artifacts. It'll wow you. Go through their art gallery, and you'll be more proud to be an American. It shows what can happen with free enterprise around the world.

When she was nineteen months old, Helen Keller had a disease that left her deaf and blind. Luckily her teacher, Annie Sullivan, saw more in this little girl than she saw in herself or anyone else saw in her. She ran water over this crippled girl's hands and tapped into her hand, the word W-A-T-E-R, W-A-T-E-R, 157 times. When Helen Keller got it, she showed the world how anyone could not only overcome their adversities but accomplish great things, all because of a mastermind. Each and every one of us has the possibility of having a team and achieving their dream. Individuals—maybe you— have within you the Annie Sullivan touch to take others out of their handicaps, limitations, blindness, sickness, or problems, if you just try. I am giving you absolute permission forever to release the splendor within others that they do not now know that they have. You can do it—uniquely, transformatively, and inevitably.

I have a friend named Betty Tisdale. She read a story once about a man who went to Vietnam during the height of the war, when the Vietnamese hated the war so much that, wearing black silk outfits, they strapped their kids to their back and were going over the Himalayas. A lot of the parents unfortunately froze to death, leaving instant orphans.

This man, Tom Dooley, was a medical doctor. He had a little bit of affluence and opened up eight orphanages in South Vietnam. Betty Tisdale saw him on TV one night. She was a secretary who worked for Senator Jacob Javits. She came to lunch every day with a brown bag, saved all her money for fifty weeks in a row, and bought a ticket to Vietnam because she wanted to go see if this orphanage story was true.

When she got to one of the orphanages, in Saigon, she was astounded. It touched her heart. She said, "I want to adopt every one of these kids."

"Betty," they said, "we'd love for you to adopt every one of these kids, but you've got to be married first."

"OK, I'll go home and think about it."

That night Betty meditated and prayed, asking, "Who would my ideal husband be?" She visualized that her ideal husband would be a pediatrician.

The next day she went to the military base and met a pediatrician, Dr. Patrick Tisdale, who had just moved in. He was a widower with five kids. Within two days, he was on his knees, saying, "Please, Betty. Marry me."

"I'll let you marry me under one circumstance," she replied: "If you'll allow me to adopt two Vietnamese kids."

He agreed. They were called back to the United States, and because of Betty's love and affection for the kids, the orphanage called her up and said, "The war has heated up here. We have 419 refugee kids. We have nowhere to put them. Do you think you can get them adopted? You've got such a great heart."

Betty put her hand over the phone and said to her husband, "Would you let me do this if I can get them back?"

"I'm sure we could get them adopted," he said. "Go at it."

She called up the president of United Airlines and explained her problem. He replied, "Thank you for calling me first. I didn't plan on helping you out, but I'll fly home all those kids for you at no charge."

"Oh, thank you," she said.

"By the way, Ms. Tisdale, do you have a flight over and back?"

"No, my husband and I weren't planning on this, and I don't have any money saved."

"All the tickets will be at the airport for you tomorrow."

Betty got to Saigon and started to load the kids on a plane. Sure enough, the battle got white-hot again. They wouldn't let her fly out.

"Why not?" she asked.

"Because we don't let commercial planes fly through war areas. It's not a good idea to blow $170 million planes out of the air or kill innocent civilians."

Now Betty had all the kids and nowhere to go, and she didn't know how long the war was going to stay white-hot.

Betty went back into meditation and said, "OK. I've got it." She went to the office of the four-star general in command. The secretary said, "You don't have an appointment. He's running a hot war. His goal is to keep men and women soldiers alive. I'm sorry, Ms. Tisdale, I can't help you."

Betty went back over to the corner, prayed and meditated again, and said, "OK. I've got it." She walked up to the general's secretary and said, "Is the general's mom still alive?"

"She is."

"Here's my telephone credit card. Would you please get her on the phone?"

When she got the general's mother on the line, Betty said, "From the heart of one mother to the heart of another mother, your son's doing exactly what he's supposed to be doing—taking care of soldiers. That's his mission, but from my heart to your heart, I need your son to airlift these kids from here to Bangkok, where United Airlines will fly them back to the United States. As one mother to another, will you help me?"

The general's mother said, "Put my son on the phone."

The son got on the phone, and his mother said, "Boy, if you ever want to come to Thanksgiving at my house again, you will meet now with Mrs. Tisdale and figure out how to airlift those kids out of Saigon. Have I made myself abundantly clear, boy?"

"Yes, mommy."

Betty loaded these kids onto the plane. Up to that point, they had probably only seen American military blowing their parents away. They had never seen a diaper or a bottle, let alone the inside of a plane.

They were getting onto the plane, and Betty thought she was home free. But anytime you have a big goal, you've got to have a team to get your dream together, because at the eleventh hour something is going to come up that will stifle and stop you unless you have your team together.

A doctor showed up from social services and said, "Betty, you can have all those orphan kids if you've got their birth certificates." You may not have your birth certificate available—I know I don't—but no refugee kid has a birth certificate with them.

Betty said, "I'm sorry; I forgot them. You wait right here."

Betty knew her way intimately around pediatrics, and she knew her way around Saigon. She ran to the nearest hospital, went to pediatrics, and talked the people there into creating birth certificates.

In a flash, they were creating false birthdays, birth dates, sexes, geographies for all these kids. In twenty minutes, she came back with the ink still smearing on those certificates. The doctor looked at it and said, "Looks like it's in order to me. You're out of here."

Betty got all the kids back and got all of them adopted.

Thirty years later, Jack Canfield and I are in Seattle, Betty's hometown, selling books. She shows up again; I hadn't seen her for years. She hugs me and kisses me with tears in her eyes and hands me a letter. She says, "You know, Mark, I just went back to Saigon thirty years later, and I got a picture of the kids I couldn't take, and here's that picture."

The kids were forlorn. Most of them had rotten teeth and weakened bodies. She said, "Then I had a meeting for all the ones that I brought here and got adopted. As you know, we adopted several of the kids ourselves.

"This little girl wrote us a letter and asked us to give it to you. I gave every one of them your book, because it's meant so much to me."

The letter read:

Dear Mark and Jack, I arrived here at two years old, and I didn't know that Betty Tisdale had gone through fiery hoops and moved mountains to save my measly little life. In my whole life here, I've been ashamed to be a Vietnamese-American. Now that I've read what Betty Tisdale did to save my life and I see that I could have been one of those kids that didn't get here, I am, first of all, proud to be Vietnamese, second of all, proud to be an American, and third, thankful that somebody like Betty Tisdale came out of her heart.

She was willing to start with no resources except a dream team alliance with her husband. She had a big dream and enrolled a lot of people, an airline, and an entire country to adopt us. You've changed my whole understanding of life and how to live and live with honor and dignity, and I just want to say thank-you.

EIGHT

Achieving Total Well-Being

Let's talk about achieving total well-being. It's never too late to rebuild your body to make it healthy. It's fun to be fit, think right, eat right, live right, do right, and discipline yourself to do things that have multiple payoffs.

"Do something new every day for the next thirty days," says Maxwell Maltz, author of *Psycho-Cybernetics*, "and it'll become a habit—a habit that's harder *not* to do on the thirty-first day than it is to do." For example, if you have not been doing push-ups, start by doing one simple push-up the first day. Do two the second day. By day thirty you will do thirty push-ups consistently and more easily than you did one the first day. Make it a lifelong habit whether you're a male or a female.

Most addictions are considered bad, but I'm trying to get you to have addictions to good habits, what psychiatrist Bill Glasser calls positive addictions. Great thinking, a really good diet, complete nutraceuticals, adequate daily sleep, exercise, a positive mental attitude, and a new commitment will refresh your sense of well-being. Small illnesses will disappear, and the big ones will diminish. Instead of having to focus so much energy on keeping well and maintaining health, you'll be in good health; it'll be second nature to you.

Waking up to new levels of physicality will wake us up to new levels of emotionality, and we'll be in more balance. We'll reach new levels of mentality and spirituality as well.

Discipline in any one area cascades through the other areas of life. Good health not only leads to a feeling of well-being but enables us to maintain balance throughout our entire lives.

Total well-being can be defined as pursuing appropriate goals in all areas of life. Health is a matter of staying within an ideal body weight, taking in sound nutrition, maintaining a systematic physical fitness program, using a stress-reduction technique like meditation, having a sense of play in life, learning how to increase longevity—"to be ageless and timeless," as author Deepak Chopra says—and rewarding ourselves with a high level of freedom from pain.

We're not going to change our diet or add exercise to our regime unless we see immediate personal benefits. To begin with, decide exactly what you want from your changes. Here are some suggestions. Do you want a trimmer, flatter stomach? Rippling, well-defined muscles? Freedom from smoking, drinking, and drugs? A lower heart rate? Lower cholesterol? Lower fat intake? A body in better condition, with more flexibility and better internal monitoring of your feelings? To live without aging? You can get older without getting old. You can experience nearly pain-free living.

I read an article about Sophia Loren when she was in her upper sixties. She wouldn't even let herself think she was in pain when she was getting out of a chair. I thought, "What a brilliant insight." As a result, she feels really good about herself.

We all want one or more of the above. So what are you waiting for? What is your definition of well-being in your own eyes?

Close your eyes for a second and visualize your highest level of well-being. How are you walking, talking, moving? What is the presence of your being? Write out what you see, feel, and believe about wellness for you. Choose at least one personal goal for enhanced well-being per month. Ask yourself, "What am I doing today, now, to move me closer to my accomplished desire of total well-being?"

Physicians take many health measurements to determine how well you are. The following five can give you a good start. Before embarking on your fitness program, check with your physician or a competent health professional, and get their approval.

1. What's your resting heart rate? The lower it is, the better. Fit Olympic athletes average as low as thirty-six beats per minute, so make it a goal to lower it, maybe by two resting heartbeats a minute. Make your commitment known to somebody else who will ask you about it; ask them to do the same with you, because it's nice to have a little competition here.

You take your pulse at your neck, at your wrist, or behind your knee. Use a clock or a stopwatch with a sweeping second hand on it, and there'll be less room for error. Count your pulse beats for six seconds and multiply the number by ten: that's your heart rate. If your pulse rate is seven beats in six seconds, you multiply it by ten, so it's seventy beats a minute, which is average. Your goal on this one is to be below average.

The best time to discover your resting pulse rate is just after a good night's sleep, upon awakening and before getting out of bed.

2. What's your recovery rate? Recovery rate is the number of minutes it takes to get back to a resting heart rate after vigorous aerobic exercise, whether it be one, two, ten, fifteen minutes. The faster you recover, the more fit you are. That's why I love exercising six or seven days a week. Your fitness builds with regular aerobic exercise. Throw in cross-training. Once in a while, include wind sprints or spinning classes so you really get going.

3. What is your percentage of body fat? Your desirable weight is the weight at which you feel well, look well, are alert, and resist fatigue and infection, and your immune system strong enough to fight off any attack. A more accurate method is determined by the actual percentage of body that is fat. The ideal for women is 23 percent, for men 15 percent. You can do this with a $10 body fat caliper. Covert Bailey, author of *Fit or Fat*, is at the leading edge of this approach, using underwater immersion to maximize the accuracy of the findings. You may or may not want to do that, but it's available at lots of different places, such as universities and health clubs.

4. How flexible are you? Can you comfortably touch your toes, do a deep knee bend, or sit in a cross-legged posture? To find out, gently and slowly try doing these things. If you find they're difficult or impossible, don't

panic. No matter what your age is, you can gently, moderately, and progressively stretch and loosen yourself again. In India, they taught me that every inch you can't touch the ground when you bend over means ten years off your life.

Celebrities like Raquel Welch, who looks beautiful inside and out, manifest maximum flexibility. She, like many others, does an hour and a half of yoga a day. If you never take any yoga class, why not make it one of your 101 goals?

5. What is your fun level? We all need to play and laugh, have a sense of whimsy and spontaneity—in other words, having fun. All of us need more fun in our lives, because we get swept up in being a parent or a worker. I'm asking you to get swept up in making work, parenting, and spiritual growth fun; make everything you do fun. Are you getting enough fun out of your life? Fun constitutes an exercise not only for the body but for the mind as well.

Laughter alone gives us a whole-body exercise. It relieves tension, and it revitalizes us. The late Dr. Norman Cousins, editor of *Saturday Review* magazine and author of *Anatomy of an Illness* and *Healing the Heart*, described how he was pulled back from death by laughter, with a little help from vitamin C. When he was told he was dying, he studied wellness, which at the time was basically unknown in the medical community. He watched all the funniest films and literally laughed his way out of disease. Ultimately he taught healing with humor to medical students at UCLA. I gave him a giant award for his life-generating healing from humor at the Inside Edge in Los Angeles in the early nineties.

If we have excellent attitudes, our lives will be filled with joyous laughter. If they aren't, we have to work on this, because most of us have been taught to get serious about being serious. Get serious about having fun. Have a sense of play. Have a kid's sense of spontaneity. Make it a goal. If you don't have a good sense of humor or a play partner in your life, get one.

How many times a day do you have fun? Count them up. Before you go to sleep at night, close your outer eyes, look inside your mind, and review the whole day. Did you have a blast? Did you laugh, chortle, jiggle, and have a sense of whimsy? Hopefully you'll find at least ten incidents a day. If it's less than ten, you're laugh- and fun-deprived. Lighten up. Be less serious. Be serious about what you're doing, but not about who you are. Have fun and whimsy.

If you take the above test, you'll probably find that you need improvement. The good news is, you're in the majority.

Now I'm asking you to get totally fit. Ask yourself, what is my potential for being totally fit? Everyone wants to get fit, but most of us never quite make it. What's your problem? Whatever the problem is, there's a solution. It's my formula to feel fit inside so that it shows on the outside. Try, and let yourself get into it.

Choose an Exercise Program

The first step in getting fit is selecting the right exercise program for you. There are all sorts available, and most of them are excellent. You can pick walking, swimming, jogging, roller-blading, roller-skating, ice skating, aerobics, treadmills, or cross-training. You can jump rope, which is great. You can even carry your jump rope with you when you travel.

You can also do trampolining, which, according to the U.S. Air Force, is one of the most effective techniques for cleaning out your lymphatic system, which is the sewer system of the body, and that's part of the healing process. We hear about so many people having lymphoma and other lymphatic system breakdowns. It is important to have a bounce-around, I believe, in every home.

It's preferable to exercise and cross-train daily to keep the body in great shape. If you're forty or over, the aim is an hour a day, six days a week.

Next, exercise with somebody. It makes it more fun to be in an environment with somebody you like. Often it's possible to combine your exercise program with somebody else's.

I love jogging with my wife and family. Early on, when my daughters were babies, I would strap them into a Snugli baby carrier on my back or on my front, or I would use a three-wheel jogging pushcart.

It's nice to exercise with your spouse and kids. I encourage you to walk at least a half-hour a day for exercise with the person of your heart's desire. It has health benefits and also provides a subconscious feeling of connection, which will put you two on a closer basis.

When I'm on the road—which millions of Americans are every day—and my energy is lackluster, occasionally I have to fantasize that I'm running with one of my friends or colleagues or family members; it keeps my mind going. I run an imaginary conversation, or I put on a headset. I recommend this to you; it makes your exercise time as painless as possible because your mind is working on something else. You set your pace at the level that you want, so you're pushing the edge of the envelope.

The ultimate exercise program is to get it your head so that you get it in your body and it's effortless effort. As Covert Bailey says, "If you really want to do it right, get fit, then diet. Most people diet first and then exercise."

Change Your Diet

Being overweight is like carrying around a knapsack of fat. My friend Pete Strudwick, who was a Thalidomide baby and was born with just two fingers and stumps on his hand and stumps for feet, is a mountain marathoner. When we were sitting at dinner one time, he pointed out that if you're only one pound overweight and you run one mile, you've carried the equivalent of one extra ton of weight. Is it a good idea to melt off that weight in your body? The answer is yes and yes.

The counterbalancing force is a sensible diet combined with a program of regular exercise. Most people become more and more sedentary as they grow older, but as we age, we need to get more exercise, not less.

Cutting back on calories and junk food is hard for all of us to do, especially as you progress in business: you get invited out to more places that have delicacies and delights that are no good for your body. Think it through, maintain balance, and have a moderate diet. It also helps to hang out with fit people who are health nuts and aware of phenomenal nutrition and who will cheer you on to your best level of health ever.

Next, rethink your ideas about food. People who, after a holiday binge at Thanksgiving or Christmas, say, "I gained 5 pounds over the weekend," either are kidding themselves or don't know what they're talking about. Since 1 pound of fat represents 3,500 calories of intake, to gain 5 pounds would mean consuming 17,500 calories over a single weekend. Impossible, or almost. That gain came from a long-term pattern of overeating. Remember, if you eat an extra 100 calories a day over a year, you gain 10 pounds. Your body, like a bank, works on the basis of deposits and withdrawals. I'm cheering you on for exercising withdrawals and slowing down on deposits a little bit.

Finally, avoid the mindset that tells us we need to lose a lot of weight quickly. If somebody has a large weight loss in a short period of time, it's usually only water loss. To lose 1,500 calories a day requires an hour and a half of jogging at 6.5 miles an hour, which is a high rate of speed.

Smart people start their diet at the supermarket, because you can't eat what you don't buy. I'm asking you to eat right. Eat a diet consisting of 70 percent live, fresh, organic fruits and vegetables. If you just remember that, you're home free. Eating live foods will replenish, revitalize, and reinvigorate your body. You can even grow your own produce and pick it right off the vine. As comedian Dick Gregory said, "The closer to the vine, the more alive it is every time."

Maintain it, don't regain it. The real objective of a sensible, lifelong plan of exercise and diet is to stay healthy, not to get sick and then get healthy again.

Remember, it's much easier and more effective to maintain good health than regain it once it's lost. If your stomach could talk, it would probably say, "I just digest it. You eat it." If we control our appetite, we control our lives. The trouble is, most of us allow our taste buds to control our eating and hence our lives.

Here are some sensible, well thought out tips that I'd like to share with you; you can accept them or not as you choose.

Decrease surplus food at meals. Decide in advance how much you want on your plate. One friend started cutting the amount of food on his plate in half and would not let himself have extra. Smart idea.

Don't snack ritualistically. It's easy to get in front of the television and start snacking. This beats up your discipline. If you must snack, avoid high-calorie snacks.

Avoid socializing in eating areas, except with the family at dinnertime. That stimulates your appetite.

Avoid white sugar, white flour, and white salt.

Eat slowly. Masticate, chew. All of us have heard that you're supposed to chew your food twenty-six times before you swallow it. The more you chew, the better, because it's that much easier for your stomach to digest. Most of us have little digestive issues as we mature.

Visualize your fitness many times a day. Imagine a picture of yourself at your ideal weight. Jack Canfield has a picture of himself at his ideal weight on the mirror, so he looks at it when he's shaving. He sees it a couple of times a day, and it keeps him pressing on. My cliché is, what you impress, you express. Each time you start to eat something, imagine your ideal weight and ask yourself, "Will this help me achieve and maintain my ideal weight?" If the answer is no, forgive yourself, but don't eat it.

Remember, there is a habit of self-sabotaging decisions here, and you can break it. All of us have stress, which sometimes leads to compulsive eating or drinking, which in turn leads to obesity and physical inactivity and more stress.

You can control the cycles in your life. You create your own fitness. You create your own diet and the length and enjoyment of your life. If fat is a symptom of being overweight, it's not the cause, it's a result. Go back to cause, which is exercise and smart eating.

Use Affirmations

Next, work on a desired result. Total well-being, not just the absence of sickness and disease, is a lifelong objective, and results are your guide. You know what you really believe not by words but by deeds. You may say you want to lose weight, but your subconscious only believes your activities, not your mere intention.

Are you thinking fit, eating less, exercising more? Your belief is visible in the results. Here are some affirmations I'd recommend to motivate yourself. Make a point of saying them often, particularly before, during, and after exercise.

I'm responsible for my own health.

My daily health habits create my good health.

I'm vibrantly healthy in spirit and body.

I'm totally well and staying that way all the days of my life.

I feel totally alive and inspire others to feel the same way.

Get a Support Team

Achieving maximum well-being is a long and permanent road. This isn't a sprint, it's a marathon, and it requires a considerable amount of support. Developing a support team should become a prime consideration along the way. Look for fit friends who are ready, willing, and able to support you to the max.

I'm a long-distance bicyclist. I do fifty, sometimes a hundred miles on Saturday and Sunday. There are only going to be a few people like that, but I have some friends who are great thinkers and like to support me. You need that kind of person.

Hear your doctor say, "You're at your ideal body weight, with a perfect pulse rate and perfect shape at the right cholesterol. It's a new you. Congratulations."

It will delight you in future months to actually say to yourself, "I knew I could do it. I said I could do it, and then I did."

One last time: the aim is total well-being. As I mentioned at the beginning of the chapter, health is only one element of well-being, albeit the most important one. Good health allows us to balance our lives, gives us energy, and moves us toward new prosperity. It enables us to give and receive love and enhance our mental, social, and spiritual growth. I see you living your dream of total well-being. In advance, let me say congratulations.

NINE

Awaken Your Spirit

Each and every one of us has a deep inner spiritual core. All of us at one time or another have felt an unexplained yearning inside that calls for fulfillment. That is our spiritual nature, asking to be recognized and integrated into our daily lives. Most of us are too busy creating outward success in our lives to pay much attention to that spiritual yearning, and yet it is important not only to recognize who we are in our depths, but also to put our spiritual nature to work for ourselves.

In work, in finance, in health, in most areas of our lives, we use terms that we all recognize and agree upon. Yet when it comes to spirituality, frequently there's a disagreement about terminology. To some, it means going to church. To others, it brings to mind a bunch of people sitting around a table, holding hands, and trying to contact the spirits of dead people. That's not what I'm talking about.

To me, spirituality involves an aspect of the self that is more than the mind or the intellect. As I've suggested, your spiritual core can be recognized by a nameless yearning for fulfillment. It involves your soul and the very heart of your being. I'm not speaking of religion or religious dogma. I believe that religions can address the spiritual, but that's not always necessarily the case. Sometimes awakening our spiritual nature is as simple as having a desire to do so. For others, it may come about because of a traumatic experience.

My teacher Buckminster Fuller had his spiritual awakening during his bleakest hour. His business had failed. One of his daughters had died, and he felt that he was at fault. His whole world crashed down upon him, and the intellectual community ostracized him. His wife's family and many others considered him nothing more than a Yankee tinkerer. One cold, blustery night, he decided to end his life. He left his apartment and walked out to the edge of Lake Michigan. With every intention of casting himself into the turbulent waters, he stood at the lakeside for hours, thinking about his life. He asked himself, "Is there a God? Do I, Buckminster Fuller, have a reason and purpose for this life that I now possess?"

Within his own heart and soul, he had this answer: "There's an a priori intelligence in the universe that works for good, and your job is to dedicate yourself to humanity's comprehensive welfare on Spaceship Earth." All thoughts of suicide vanished as he realized that his life was not to be cast aside.

An a priori intelligence is a causeless cause or, by any one of innumerable names, God, who created the entire universe and each of us. We each have an intrinsic spark of divinity that needs, wants, and during times of torment and travail demands recognition. It is sometimes called the still, small voice. Bucky needed it and got it to answer. It is available to each and every one of us, whether we have ever called upon it or not. It is there awaiting your sincere request. You will be heard and answered.

Each and every one of us belongs to a greater purpose, and this is where we have to fulfill that purpose. Bucky never stopped or swayed from the unfolding of his spiritual purpose from that day forward. He wrote forty masterful books and developed many major inventions, like geodesic domes, Dymaxion cars, Dymaxion maps, and floating cities. I worked with him on a concept called "World Game," which was about how to make the world work for 100 percent of humanity, making every one economically and physically successful. These ideas still excite me, and I hope you'll read his brilliant thinking in his book *Utopia or Oblivion*. Bucky was unequivocally a human treasure, the Leonardo da Vinci of our time.

My own spiritual awakening was long in coming. As a child, my family attended an orthodox church in the Midwest. Everyone, including my dad, who worked eighteen hours a day, came to the sermons. They were so humdrum and boring that my dad used to snore his way through them, which always embarrassed my mom, my brothers, and myself. We'd hit him and say, "Wake up, Dad. Wake up." He'd say, "What happened? What happened?" My belief was that religion was something that put people to sleep. You went to get your siesta and your chill-out time.

When I talked to my friends about the church, our common experience was that it told us, "Don't do this. Don't do that." Consequently, our experiences were essentially negative and unfulfilling. Our early consensus was that maybe we didn't need to get involved in that aspect of our lives.

Then, very shortly after I went bankrupt, two of my friends invited me to attend a church to hear a famous minister, Dr. Norman Vincent Peale, at New York's Marble Collegiate Church, at Fifth Avenue and 29th Street. It was a whole new experience for me. I was intellectually stimulated while being spiritually uplifted. The minister wanted to love people into heaven. What a concept! He fed his congregation spiritual vitamins. He infused them with vital, life-giving enthusiasm. His sermon made me aware of a spiritual void in my life that I desperately needed and wanted to fill.

Afterward my friends took me to lunch. Then, for kicks, they suggested we go to another church up in Harlem. When we arrived, I was astounded to see so many elegant, chauffeur-driven limousines and Rolls-Royces bringing in congregants. Once inside, I found that the environment was a strange combination of lavish opulence and tasteful reverence. This church was filled to overflowing with over five thousand worshipers. We were three white men in a predominantly black church. We were accepted, hugged, loved, kissed, and welcomed. No one knew or cared that I'd gone bankrupt a few days earlier.

The minister, Dr. Frederick Eikerenkoetter, better known as Reverend Ike, began to speak. He lit my spiritual spark plug. Remember, this was three in the afternoon. He provided me with exciting new insights about abundance, right thinking, and letting hope take one forward. I discovered that my bankruptcy had put my mind, spirit, and soul in bondage. I wanted to be free spiritually and economically. He said, "God is rich. He created the universe and all that's in it. God is infinite possibility in action. You have God within you, so you have infinite creative possibilities within you."

I could feel the spirit moving within me. I recognized these words as truth, and the truth would set me free. My spiritual nature was to awaken for the first time, and I was on my way to living a more spiritual life.

The awakening of our spiritual nature, no matter what the circumstance, is always a precursor to future greatness. I have seen it in such leaders as Albert Einstein, Abraham Lincoln, Ralph Waldo Emerson, Martin Luther King Jr., Albert Schweitzer, Buckminster Fuller, Mother Teresa, and thousands of others. Each felt a spiritual awakening and believed that the greater force that operates spiritually in the universe directed his or her accomplishments. They felt they could personally tap into that force and use it to better the world. It's what I would call a sense of destiny, which, I believe, is coded into you, me, and everyone, and it's just waiting for us to awaken it.

We can do a number of things to add a sense of spirituality to our lives. They're simple, yet the results will help bring harmony and balance to all other aspects of our lives.

Look for a minister, priest, rabbi, or great spiritual teacher to facilitate your spiritual growth. Make sure they are growing and that their congregation is growing too. That's a pretty sure sign of health. I like to use the line from Dr. Norman Vincent Peale: "We're grow-ing like a rabbit farm on a hormone diet."

If the power of attraction, the enthusiasm, is there, the spirit within is showing without. The last letters of *enthusiasm* are I-A-S-M: *I am soul myself* (or *I am sold myself*). If you're convinced, you're convincing. If they've got the juice, they can help you get to your juice.

I've never met a truly great person who didn't have a great, inspiring spiritual mentor. Bucky Fuller told me that when he met Albert Einstein, Einstein glowed with the spiritual life that emanated from his countenance, even though he had one shoe on with a sock and the other shoe on without a sock. At that time Bucky had published his first great work: *4D Time Lock*. Einstein had read what Bucky had writ-ten. He said, "Young man, you absolutely amaze me. I never thought anyone would come up with a practical application for $E = MC2$ during my lifetime." Then he hugged and kissed him on the cheek in the European congratulatory fashion.

Another time Bucky had to meet Einstein, but Bucky got caught in traffic. When he arrived, he almost wanted to get down on his hands and knees and apol-ogize for being late. But Einstein said, "It makes no dif-ference. What I do I can do waiting for you, Dr. Fuller. In the universe there is no time or space; these are man-made concepts and constructions."

Einstein was so compassionate and generous because of his understanding of the universe. He believed that there has to be a God, because everything is in perfect placement. Einstein was profoundly in tune with the universe and with God. That's why he was a great and inspiring teacher.

When you select your spiritual teacher, match your feeling nature with that of the teacher. Do you resonate core to core, spirit to spirit? Do they have the values and qualities you are aspiring to? Do they inspire the presence of the spirit within to emanate out? Go to somebody. Listen to what they say. Does it light your inner light? Does it turn you on? Does it make you resonate at a higher vibration? Do you feel it in the music and the chorus and see it in the people? Are they all alive and growing and thriving?

If, after your experience with that teacher, you feel less human or you find the experience boring, he or she is not the right one for you. If you cannot have a direct experience of a teacher, listen to some audios or read some of the classic books. Check out a couple of different dimensions. Send out your inner spiritual radar; all of a sudden it'll start going beep, beep, beep, and you'll get on course to your higher spirituality, because there's somebody out there that can ignite your spiritual spark plugs and turn your spiritual engine on.

Hang out with people who feel and believe as you do spiritually. Have an ongoing communication with like-minded people in order to keep your spiritual life going and glowing. No log burns alone. Stimulating conversations of a spiritual nature will keep you in tune. My wife and I have daily communication about our shared beliefs and how our lives revolve around those beliefs. I know this makes our marriage stronger and better in all ways. We launch our days with an hour of prayer and meditation. We harmonize and agree to having every day be a great, productive, inventive, and profitable day, when we each serve greatly with love.

Also express gratitude in all that you do. I believe that gratitude is one of the highest spiritual principles. Before you get up, start your day in a positive, uplifting way. Express your gratitude the first thing every morning. Likewise, express gratitude for a day well done right before you go to sleep at night, and you will have pleasant dreams.

There's so much to be thankful for, and the more you're thankful for, the more you get to be thankful for. Be thankful that the sun comes up day in, day out; you can set your clocks to it. Astronomers do exactly that.

Say an original grace, while holding hands with your companions, over every meal. Maybe even rub your hands, run them out the outside of the food, and say, "All this food, good, safe, to my nourishment." Expressing gratitude for food uplifts the spirit and makes the meal taste better; the newest research says it will even make it safer.

I had stomach poisoning twice in my life before I learned this technique, which makes a brilliant amount of sense to me. It may just be that my inner thoughts now say, "Don't eat that asparagus or that apple, because it's bad." Let your intuition and your deep feeling nature be your guide here.

I really believe in saying grace while holding hands with the others at the table, and we practice it just about everywhere I go. I believe that it not only helps you to avoid indigestion but makes the food safer and more nourishing to your body. I thank God for all the people who have contributed to the food in front of me—the farmer who grew it, the people who processed it and transported it, and those who prepared it for my consumption.

Look around you and notice all the wonderful things the universe has in store for you. Express your gratitude on a daily basis. We hear constantly about negative things from TV, radio, and newspapers. Challenge yourself to find gratitude everywhere. Once you start looking for the good in life, more good will start to appear, and you'll have unlimited possibilities to be grateful for.

Giving is also extremely important. Magnanimously social, it can also have immediate personal benefits. One thing you can do is give your used clothing and household items to a charity. There are many organizations such as Goodwill, Salvation Army, thrift stores, and others that can put your used items to good use. Or find a homeless shelter in your area that can use the items for those who are in desperate need right now. There are also organizations that give business clothing to people who are in the job market and trying to get off welfare.

You can deduct a portion of your charitable giving for income taxes. (Take a picture of it, because the IRS may want to see the bag of clothes that you've given.)

Go through all the clothes in your closet with yellow stickies, and rate them on a scale of one to ten—ten being you like it, love it, it has spiritual value to you—down to one. If anything rates less than a seven, give it away. There's a vacuum law of prosperity here: nature abhors a vacuum, so the minute you give something away, new things will show up in wondrous, bountiful, surprising, and exciting ways.

In addition, give back to your source of spiritual good. Give 10 percent of your wealth to your church, synagogue, or temple. This is called tithing. If 10 percent seems too high, begin with some smaller percentage. Start at 1 percent or one quarter of 1 percent, and then build up. You'll be amazed at how abundance starts to flow towards you.

Also give to a charity that winds your clock. Author Jim Rollins wisely says, "Take a little step towards God, and God takes a God-sized step towards you." Save 10 percent, as I said earlier. Tithe 10 percent. Third, plan to invest 10 percent of your money. If you make an unconscionable amount of money, you'll have more to give away.

This is worthy of a little soul searching and profound reflection. As an example, a portion of our profits from the Chicken Soup for the Soul books have been sourced to the American Red Cross; the Arbor Foundation, for which we planted 200,000 trees; the Literacy Volunteers of America; Feed the Children; Save the Children; Childhelp.org; the Horatio Alger Association of Distinguished Americans, which provides scholarships to universities or trade schools for at-risk children; and Union Rescue Mission, among others. Inside each book, we list whom we have chosen to work with, to share with, and to serve.

Work with local charities and organizations. Once you start to eradicate lack, limitations, problems, and crime closest to home first, it will extend further out, nationally and internationally.

Find your spiritual purpose and dedicate it to service in your life. A merely self-serving purpose in life is self-defeating. We must all develop our own spiritual purpose—and it's got to be bigger than ourselves—by serving others.

We see a perfect example of service in children in the Special Olympics. Many times during this event, when a child who is running in first place falls down, his friends stop, turn around, pick him up, and carry him over the finish line. Everybody gives a standing ovation because of the compassion and the cooperation and the love. If you've never attended the Special Olympics, put it on your list of goals. It'll bolster your courage and love and generosity of spirit; maybe you'll even want to help out at one of the events.

Find an organization or a movement or a spiritual group where you want to be in service to others in a way that will inspire you to be all that you can be spiritually. There are many fine organizations and movements that need you.

The hospice movement inspires me. It is founded on the belief that no one should die alone. In the book *Closer to the Light*, Dr. Melvin Morse writes about people who have had near-death experiences. They've been on a coma or briefly pronounced clinically dead, only to be revived. In each case, they report seeing the light on the other side. When this happens, everyone who is present shares the experience. It strengthens their faith and their sense of spiritual reality.

I believe that at death we make a transition into another phase of life. It loosens us and makes us more free, like taking off a tight shoe. I draw strength from that belief. If I didn't feel this, it would be an empty spot inside of me, a spiritual vacuum that would continually suck energy from me.

The hospice movement acknowledges that death is part of the life continuum. Becoming a volunteer in a local hospice will bring you closer to a spiritual understanding of life and death. It'll free your mind from the fear of death and give you energy to embrace life.

Let me conclude with a story of a friend of mine. This man was one of our great decathlon athletes and a winner in the highest sense. His name was Milt Campbell. If you have ever been to the Olympics or even watched them on TV, you've seen that Olympians do things for each other that nobody else would do. Milt is black. He was in Sydney, Australia, and he'd won nine of the ten events.

In the decathlon, one event comes on top of another, so by the time Milt was ready to do his tenth event, he had melted down. Milt was black. There was a British participant who didn't like—back then the term was "colored folks"—so he didn't like Milt at all.

As the events progressed, the British Olympian saw Milt's love and the desire and how he had kept telling himself, "I can do it. I can do it. I can do it," and he was affirming with Milt. They competed against each other, but this guy didn't have a chance, and if Milt got it, he would win. They were running against each other in the last event of the decathlon.

Milt's energy was grounding to a halt and slowing him down. The British runner, who started out not liking him but now loved and appreciated him, came running up to Milt, put his hand around his waist, and literally thrust him across the finish line ahead of everyone else, so Milt won a decathlon gold medal for America.

Milt didn't expect this, and it caused tears to run down his cheeks. His rival started out hating him but was turned around by seeing the truth of his being and realizing that he deserved to win the decathlon, so he helped Milt fulfill his dream.

I was blessed to travel around doing seminars with Milt. His profound spirit inspired listeners at the depth of their souls to have courage to compete at higher and more exalted levels and to believe they could win against the odds.

The point is that you're here, and I'm daring you to live your dreams. When you start to do so, somebody else is going to see your dream and come up unexpectedly, just as that other runner did for Milt. A lot of people out there may resist you, resent you, be jealous of you, put you down, but in the final analysis, one of them may come out of nowhere and help you cross the finish line.

TEN

Ten Instant Steps to Success

The ten instant principles to success I'm going to teach you in this chapter have worked for a cab driver, they've worked for a president of the United States, they've worked for a college professor. They'll work for anyone if you just apply them.

Why? We're dealing with principles, and principles always work. Gravity is a principle that always works. Your foot always goes down to the floor when you wake up in the morning. Principles are impersonal. They're weightless. They're timeless. They're ageless. It's like two times two, which always equals four. They'll never change. They don't wear out, rust out, or get tired.

These principles will work for you. They'll take you to heights beyond your imagination, higher than your aspiration, if you read them often enough so that they become a part of your subconscious pattern of thinking.

I'm asking you to read these principles multiple times, because the first time through, you're going to say, "No. That's too easy." The second time you read them, you'll say, "Yeah. Maybe that is true." By the third, fourth, fifth, or seventh reading, you're going to say, "I've always known that. This has always been my pattern of thinking. I've always known that I could have instant success and that I could pull off real miracles and real magic in my life." That's the category I want you to get to.

At first, it's going to be a little bit hard to believe. Everyone knows what everyone knows: you can't have instant success, any more than you can have instant healing. Yet there are many instant successes, and we're at a time of instant success, because we're in the time of the fastest change in history. We're at the time of the most abundance, the most prosperity, the greatest rise of the stock market in human history.

When we look back ten years out, I want you to say, "I read this one chapter, and it made a profound difference from the inside out. It changed my thinking, and my thinking changed my results."

I see you as an instant success. I know that sometime down the road you and I are probably going to be synchronized in time and space on an airplane, in a restaurant, or at one of my talks, and I want to hear your story of how you became an instant success.

Here are ten instant steps to success.

Ten Instant Steps to Success

1. Instant wealth.
2. Storyboard your future.
3. Acknowledge your past successes.
4. Plan your future success.
5. Set goals and objectives.
6. Overcome procrastination.
7. Act as if.
8. Be coachable.
9. Network your way to instant success.
10. Expand and contract time.

Instant Wealth

Everyone wants this, everyone dreams about it, and I'm going to tell you how to manifest it. It's called *instant wealth*. In his classic *Think and Grow Rich*, Napoleon Hill says, "When riches begin to come, they come in such avalanching, overflowing abundance, you'll wonder where they've been hiding during all the lean years."

I teach, believe, and have experienced that you are one idea away from wealth and riches. One idea can make you rich. That's right, but it's got to be the right idea, and one that you can apply instantly. The criteria I recommend are as follows, and I ask you to consider them seriously.

1. Could you start with zero or low capitalization, or at any rate with someone else's capital or technology that you can harvest for them? I'm going to give you some examples.

2. Could you have zero or low time investment? Something that doesn't take a lot of time to launch, gain momentum, and maintain.

3. Low management. You don't want to be in the management business. You want to be in the business we're going to talk about (which is number seven).

4. Low energy and effort, or better yet, somebody else's energy and effort.

5. Low risk. The more successful you are in business, the less risk you're willing to take. You don't want to go backsliding. You don't want to lower your standard of living. I'm going to teach you that it's easier to raise your

standard of living and a whole lot more fun to improve your life and lifestyle.

6. High thinking and high service. This is the game. We've gone through the Industrial Age and we've come into what I call the Thinking Age. This is where the payoff is.

7. Have high profits. Some people think high profits are a 50 percent return, but in fact the average business in America is about 4 percent profitable. The average grocery store chain is about 1 percent profitable. How do they make their money? The old joke says volume.

Yet you look around and you see that one of the richest men in the world is a software king: Bill Gates. It costs 42 cents to manufacture a piece of software, and it sells anywhere from $29 to $300. I recently got a shot for hepatitis B. Each shot costs maybe 10 cents at the most to manufacture (not counting research and development), but it cost me $90. When you start thinking about it, that is a great profit. Why not look for profits where you can really clean up?

Now I want to talk to you about profits at the of the people that *Time* magazine calls *instantaires*, which is a new form of billionaire. These are people who made software so quickly and generated so much money that they became instantly wealthy.

Jeff Bezos, of the amazing Amazon.com, created the perfect business on paper. It goes right through the seven points I've just outlined. Amazon.com is an electronic mail order catalogue that sells millions of book titles on the Internet, not to mention enormous quantities of other goods.

Jeff had one simple idea and exploited it before the multibillion-dollar bookstores like Barnes and Noble and Borders even understood what was happening. There's plenty of room in this field, as I'll show you.

Amazon.com is basically a front or a virtual company, the kind that I'm suggesting you could create. His website takes customer orders and their cash payments, and then he has somebody else do the delivery (although Amazon has been getting into direct delivery of late).

Jeff started with a brilliant idea and no capital. He saw and developed an emerging market. In May 1997, at age thirty-three, after only a few months in business, he took Amazon.com public, and his net worth eclipsed $500 million overnight. Everybody was betting against him. His stock started at $18 a share but jumped within six months to $60 a share. In 2020, he became the first person in history to be worth $200 billion. He is now running a trillion-dollar global enterprise with a subscription service called Prime, which gives free deliveries.

From a marketing point of view, Amazon is the first and the fastest, and it's so aggressive in its marketing that it now practically owns the American shopper's mindset. It just keeps expanding.

What does that mean? Think businesses are going to work. Paper businesses are going to work. Virtual companies are going to work. Intellectual properties are going to work. It's the time to let the good times roll. You can conceive, believe, and achieve instant wealth with a virtual idea. There are more emerging markets now than ever before. Why? Because there are 7.7 billion people in the world. All you have to do is turn on your awareness, tune in, keep your eyes open, and listen closely.

Opportunity is everywhere, but it always starts inside your mind. Let me take another example: Peter Lynch, superstar of the Magellan mutual fund family. He said that everybody basically buys everything at the same time. We buy our smartphones, minivans, and Nike shoes together. We all drink Starbucks coffee at the same time because it's cool, it's in, and it's chic.

My point is, get in front of a trend, or, better yet, create a trend. In cyberspace, you sell things on a computer screen; the buyers do not care where or if you exist in the physical realm, or how you obtain the goods that you sell. They just want what they want and are willing to give you electronic cash for it. Like Jeff, you get to be the middleman, the broker, the agent and make big money fast.

Jeff Bezos' mantra is GBF: *Get big fast*. When Jeff started thinking about cyberselling, he enumerated his opportunities: one, books; two, software; three, music; four, videos. Next was location. He said one ought to have proximity to high-tech talent and to be near a major book wholesaler. One should also be in a state with a small population.

Next, the company name. What's the right company name? We all have that problem. Number one, Jeff said, start with the letter A; two, convey large size; three, be short and easy to spell; and four, be internationally recognizable. Hence Amazon.com.

Where did Jeff launch his first business? In the same place as the guy who invented the pacemaker and the guys who started Hewlett Packard—in his garage. If you don't have a garage, you could start your multibillion-dollar business in your bedroom.

Storyboard Your Future

I have a great friend named Hugh. By the time he was sixty-eight, he'd gone in and out of several successful businesses, but luck turned against him and he bottomed out. He lost everything—his house, his car, and his wife. To get anywhere, he had to hitchhike or take a bus, and he was feeling downtrodden, despondent, and disconsolate.

Then all of a sudden Hugh remembered the idea that I'm going to teach you now: *storyboard your future*. Hugh got a big piece of plasterboard, cut pictures out of his favorite magazines of the places he wanted to visit, the things he wanted to do, and the person he wanted to become again. Within six months, he was back up in his luck. It's now a few years later, and I've been to his lavish house on Dana Point, California. I've driven in his brand-new Cadillac, and his former wife has remarried him.

The terrific part of this story is that every one of us can storyboard our future, and when we see it, we can do it instantly. The minute you put it on paper and take ownership of it in your mind pictorially, your image starts to manifest as your reality.

Let me take you through the seven steps of this process.

1. Get a big piece of white posterboard.

2. Write at the top, "My ideal future." Why go for less than your ideal?

3. Make sections—family, finance, career, health, social, spiritual, mental.

4. Gather your favorite magazines. I'm talking about high-class, elegant magazines, the ones that show the places that you dream of and lust for, that are lavish, opulent, extravagant—magazines like *Town and Country*, *The Robb Report*, *Architectural Digest*, *Wired* if you are into computers, *Cosmopolitan*, *Vogue*.

Now go through the magazines and cut out pictures of the advertisements. Cut out the words. Cut out the phrases, the ideas, the concepts, and the pictures. For example, if you want a car, cut out the picture of the car of your heart's desire. Let's say it's a BMW and let's say it's the big BMW, the 740i. Get it in exactly the color you want, with all the safety features. Start taking ownership.

5. Get a friend or friends who want to creatively imagine their best future and accept it into their reality instantly, because there's power and momentum in somebody else being committed to the same idea you are.

6. Schedule an uninterrupted time of three hours when you can go through the magazines with a pair of scissors and cut out the pictures of your future wardrobe, jewelry, your life, and lifestyle, as well as the words that capture the essence of the feeling that you're attempting to get. If you can get that feeling now, you can manifest it in the very near future.

7. Attractively paste, glue, or tape all these pictures in a delightful order. The more exciting they are, the more romance you can put into your creation (because your subconscious is feminine in nature), and the more you impress it on your mind, the more likely you are to express the storyboard of your future.

It's not just for my friend Hugh to come from nowhere at a mature age, regain his life, wife, status, power, and influence. You can do the same thing if you'll just storyboard the future of your heart's desire.

Acknowledge Your Past Successes

Divide your life into three basic periods, say birth to age twelve, ages thirteen to twenty-five, and from age twenty-five to the present.

Here you are acknowledging all your past successes, no matter how little, because little successes build into big successes. Little acorns become giant oaks, and big shots are little shots that keep shooting. We need to get the momentum going in your mind and remind you of how successful you are.

Let me give some examples out of my own life. In the first third, I was born. Number two, I graduated from elementary school. Almost everybody has done at least that. If you've graduated high school, graduated college, and went on for higher education, put down your highest, most plausible, and most praise-worthy credential. Number three, my parents and my brothers love me. That's a nice launch for the first third of my life.

In the second third, I created a rock group, which wowed me at the heart level. One night I was watching the Beatles on TV. I called up my buddy Gary Young-berg and said, "Gary, did you see that?"

"Man, it wowed my heart to watch those Beatles," said Gary. "They came in and shut down Kennedy Airport. They were on Ed Sullivan. Everybody in America watched it."

At the time the Beatles' big hit was "I Want to Hold Your Hand." As I look back, I see that what they were doing with that song was helping everybody over their feeling of rejection.

"So what are we going to do about it?" Gary asked.

"We're starting a rock group tomorrow."

"You can't do that."

"Why not?"

"Do you play anything?"

"No," I said, "do you?"

"No."

"Then we're qualified." I said.

"How can you say that?"

"Look at Ringo," I said. (I'm joking. Ringo is a great percussionist.)

We started a rock group called the Messengers. I had saved the money that I'd made from selling since I was a little kid, so I lent Gary money to buy an electronic organ and an electric guitar. I got a bass guitar. We got a few guys together, and in two weeks we were booked full-time in a niche market, working at YMCA sock hops at $17 an hour. All six band members made enough to go through college, buy our own cars, have our own motorcycles, and have great clothes. We had the whole life and lifestyle. For me, that was success. Then I graduated university, and number three, started my own business. That's the second third of my life.

I'm asking you to write down three successes for the first third of your life, three from the second, and three from the third.

Then write down your five-year plan. What would you like if you could have anything in the next five years? For me, it was to become a best-selling author and to have career advancement.

I'm talking about successes from a business point of view. You can do this process from a family point of view, you can do it from a parental point of view, but take the point of view you want and write out some of your successes.

Then, what would you like over the next five years? Here are a couple of choices that I think most people would go for: Number one, be financially independent and debt-free. Number two, have time freedom. I don't know what time freedom means to you, but I teach and believe in the concept of retiring now. Why not have instant success so that you can retire? For me, that means taking off a week a month, as does Jack Canfield. You decide what time freedom is for you. It may just be a four-day weekend once a month or once a quarter. It may be a week off a quarter—whatever it you want. Then you build up to it.

Fulfill Your Genius

Point number three is *fulfilling your genius*. You were here to take some genius activity to the highest heights. Why not go for it?

I'm asking you to get your mind thinking success, acting success, feeling success, and having instant success. Review your successes daily and add more. Create a victory log, a success log, something that you can look back and review. The more you think about successes, the more successes you'll have to think about.

The next part is to do a mirror exercise. Look in the mirror, look yourself straight in the eyes, and review your successes. Say, "Congratulations. You were successful. You were born and you lived." Some people don't; mortality in some countries is exceedingly high.

The mirror exercise goes straight through your pupils into the portals of your soul, so it starts to permeate the inner spaces of your mind. I'm asking you from my heart to yours to acknowledge your successes.

Then go to the next phase: acknowledge the success of your staff, your family, your teachers, your friends, your coworkers. The more you acknowledge other people's success, the more fascinated you'll become with success, and the more success you'll have to be fascinated with.

Display your own success symbols. Have pictures of you and the who's whos of the world on your walls. Hopefully you've got, or will get, a car that has some prestige. You'll win trophies and awards. Hang them up in prominent places to keep you reminded full-time of what's going right.

My friend Dr. Ken Blanchard, who wrote *The One Minute Manager*, says, "Catch people doing something right, but the most important person to catch doing something right is yourself, if you want to have instant success."

Plan Your Future Success

Instant success idea number four: *plan your future success now*. As the cliché goes, if you fail to plan, you plan to fail.

Take a piece of paper and write at the top, "My future will be happy and successful if . . ." On the left side of the paper, write down the good idea. Let's say the good idea is, "I'd like a new home." Then on the right-hand side, you write down the objective: "I want a four-thousand-square foot home that's spacious, gracious, and palatious, that is on the beach so I can wake up and have the sun caress my face and I can walk out, put my feet in the Pacific Ocean, and have the sand ooze through my feet. I'm going to have that home on the Pacific Ocean in Southern California by X date." Give yourself a little bit of time to manifest that, because it has to get inside you so you can have it in your outside experience.

Number two is "I want a vacation." That's the good idea. The objective is, "I will visit Kahuna, Hawaii, for seven days, August 15 through 22 of this year."

Now your mind starts figuring out how to accomplish this. The minute you say, "This is what I'm going to do as a good idea," and you put it down as an objective on paper—"Don't think it, ink it," is my cliché—suddenly all kinds of things start happening. You may win a trip. You may see a cost-effective trip. Your boss may say, "You've done such a superb job. Where would you like to go if you could go anywhere on vacation?"

Don't worry about the how. Your subconscious will figure that out. Just be busy with your mind business, which is planning your future in a wondrous way.

Number three: "I want a new wardrobe." I understand this from a man's point of view: "I'll go to the Bernini warehouse sale in January, and I'll invest in four new suits, two sport coats, seven ties, and four shirts." Be specific. If you go through the colors and say that they're going to be perfectly matched and that you're going to look as if you just walked out of *GQ*, all the better.

Good idea number four: "I'll lose weight." For an objective, write down exactly what your ideal weight is going to be; that you're going to have to buy new clothes; that everyone's going to come up to you and say, "Congratulations, you look like a shadow of your former self"; that you feel fit and healthy and happy; and that you look lean, trim, and ready to go into the instant future of your heart's desire.

The minute you have your plan, your success starts unfolding. We'll expand it by going into instant success idea number five.

Set Goals and Objectives

When you set goals that are outstanding, then you get to build outstanding relationships. You get to have outstanding results that have results.

I've already urged you to write down your goals and objectives and make them clear, but let me add a few more points. They've got to be believable. Believable to whom? Believable to you. They've got to be desirable—desirable to you. They've got to be things that you yourself want. A parent may want you to go to college and be a doctor, but you may not want that at all.

A dentist came to one of my seminars and said, "Until you said, 'Put what you really want down in writing,' I didn't know that I became a dentist for my mother and not for myself. I hate dentistry. I just got sued and lost $575,000 because I drilled through the side of some guy's mouth. I was desiring to be a dentist for mom, not for me."

You've got to do what you desire. What do you want in your heart of hearts? It's got to be attainable. Science fiction often becomes science fact, so you can write down some really wild ideas.

At one point rocket scientist Wernher von Braun goes to John F. Kennedy and says it is possible to land a man on the moon. Kennedy then announces to the public, "In this decade, we'll land a man on the moon." Von Braun comes back in and says, "Wait, wait, Jack. I didn't say we could do it. I said it was a good idea." Kennedy says, "Well, we've got ten years to pull it off." Because it was a big goal, it had a lot of juice, and it was measurable, we arrived on the moon in eight years and two months. If you can't measure it, you can't obtain it.

You want to set long-term, intermediate, and short-term goals. My colleague Harvey Mackay just came back from Japan and was telling me that he was with one of the greats over there. He asked him, "May I see your goals?" The man showed him a three-hundred-year goal plan. Harvey asked, "How are you going to do that?" The man replied, "Patience." Only the inscrutable Japanese mind can do something that great.

Intermediate goals are three to five years. Here's the question I'd ask if you and I were together face-to-face: if we were getting together three years from now and you had instant success, what would have had to happen to make you happy and feel fulfilled? You really want to put some juice into this and write it out.

Short-term goals are one year down to as little as one hour. You ask what you could accomplish in a year, and you break it down into monthly, then into weekly, then into daily parts. Somebody says, "I want to earn $100,000 a year." If you take out all the holidays, you work 250 days out of the year. So you've got to earn $400: $400 x 250 = $100,000. Then, as Ben Feldman pointed out, all you've got to do is take that $400 a day, add one zero, and it becomes $4,000 a day. That's $1 million a year.

I hope you'll read this multiple times, because the first time you're likely to say, "No one can earn $1 million a year." But a lot of people do. Once you start embracing the idea and grow fascinated with instant success, your radar will go out. You'll start to see that there's a lot of people doing it. Once you get the belief system that instead of being into lack, you can be into lots, loads, abundance, and plenty, you'll start setting new goals.

We want to do one-minute goal setting: in one minute you write down all the goals that you want to accomplish and then you do it the next day. Pretty soon you'll start setting more and more goals. You'll have more and more victories.

You can also do one-minute goal setting with your team or your staff. Get their actual signatures on the goals that they set, so now they're committed and you're committed. Photocopy the goals, and make sure both of you have a copy. It's even better if you can deploy it on a wall as a storyboard and look at where you want to go together. It'll amaze you what can happen.

Next thing: write out all the considerations, fears, and roadblocks related to your goals. "I would do this, but—." The game here is to get your "but" out of the way, whatever it is. "I'd do it, but I'm too afraid, or I'm too lonely, or I don't have enough courage, or I don't have enough friendship, or I'm not articulate enough." Get rid of the considerations, fears, and roadblocks by writing them down.

Here are a couple of things you can do with this list. At seminars, I have people crinkle them up and throw them at me. I say, "Now you don't have to worry about them again, because you've thrown them away." In Asia, they often take their fears to a funeral pyre and burn them right in front of the people. Now you've got no fears left, because you've just burned them away.

One of our stories in Chicken Soup tells about the time we took all the fears in a fourth-grade class—"I can't do ten pushups," "I can't get an A in math"—and went outside. We dug a hole and buried them. We rested our fears in peace. Why don't you do the same thing?

Next, write out three solutions to each one of those considerations, fears, and roadblocks. Use mind mapping: draw pictures of different ways you can get from here to there. What would it take in management, time, money, effort, and resources to reach your goal and reach it fast?

Let's also talk about compressing our goal.

I can come up with an example from my own life. When an earthquake hit at 4:31 a.m., and my whole house shook as if the *Queen Mary* had hit it, I saw my wife grab our little baby Melanie (I grabbed the bigger baby, Elizabeth). I watched her run through the dark and twilight of the early morning. She looked like Joe Montana of the 49ers carrying that kid to the safety zone, because in California houses are generally well built. Earthquakes usually don't kill people; what kills them is the shards of glass that come down as the glass warps.

It's amazing how much you can do, and you can do it in an instant if the reason is there to do it. Write down your reasons for being an instant success.

Overcome Procrastination

Point number six for becoming an instant success is *overcoming procrastination*. You may say, "But I don't procrastinate." If you say you don't procrastinate, you're probably a master at procrastination; you've just repressed the realization so long that you believe you don't.

It doesn't matter whether you believe you do or don't—all of us are masters at procrastination. I'm including myself. How do you overcome it? With a do-it-now philosophy. This is a thought affirmation that will become a superhelper as your personal motivator. You'll have to act, because "to know is to do," as the old cliché says.

Repeat this to yourself fifty times a day: "Do it now. Do it now. Do it now." Then you do it, whether it's picking up your dirty socks, polishing your car, making that telephone call, writing that business letter, or making that cold call. You know exactly what it is that you've got to do now.

In addition to affirming "Do it now," write it on some yellow stickies or three-by-five cards. Put one on the dashboard of your car. Put one on the refrigerator. Tape one onto your mirror so can you review it while you're shaving or doing your makeup.

W. Clement Stone used this affirmation daily up to last day of his life. It made him a superstar as a businessperson, as a philanthropist, and as a politico. He would always say, "Do it now." As it flashed in his mind, he went and took action, and it resulted in a lot of momentum, a lot of success, and a massive amount of influence.

Peter J. Daniels is one of the richest men in Australia. He is a speaker of great repute, and he writes books in twenty-four hours. He accumulates the information for a long time in advance; then in just twenty-four hours, he sits down and writes it. Peter started out illiterate, sick, and in poverty. When he was twenty-six, somebody read him one of the classic self-help books, and he now owns the street corners he used to fight on.

Peter is a man of great influence. He's part of the who's who of the world in overcoming many problems. He says, "Do it now" fifty times a day to himself as he's coming down the elevator from his gold penthouse in the center of Adelaide, Australia, before he gets into his gold Rolls-Royce and drives off to work. He came out of nothing and nowhere. He was a bricklayer until he learned this lesson—do it now! The minute he got that into his spirit and soul, he over-came procrastination.

It worked for Clement Stone and Peter Daniels. It's worked for me. It'll work for you if you do it. Make it a system, repeat it, review it, teach it to your family and friends, coworkers, and even your minister. Why not develop it as a success system that never fails? Then you will do it now and have instant success.

Act as If

Success point number seven: *act as if*. If you were the success you wanted to be, what would it look like, feel like, and be like from the inside out? You'd have satisfaction, and the emphasis here is on *action*. That is, if you start to act as if you were that person, you become it. The cliché on the street, of course, is, "Fake it until you make it."

That's what I did when I started speaking. I desperately wanted to speak. I attended all the speeches I could, then I went out and started selling my own speeches. I used other people's material until I could grow comfortable and confident enough to use my own. I acted as if I was going to become a great speaker, and then, hopefully, at least in my own mind, I've become one. (As the joke says, "He's a legend in his own mind.")

Let's talk about it from the point of view of literal acting. There is one man who impresses me head and shoulders above all the others as an actor: Harrison Ford. He has been in many of the top-grossing movies of all times. Harrison was working as a day carpenter for Francis Ford Coppola when he asked to be interviewed for an acting job. That started him on the road to success.

Ford became Indiana Jones, which is my favorite role that he's ever played. He drilled, practiced, rehearsed, and lived the experience from the inside out. Harrison said when he is doing a role like Indiana Jones, he becomes Indiana Jones. He thinks like him, eats like him, talks like him, lives like him. He became Indiana Jones, not once but three times.

You've got to go inside the theater of your mind and act as if you are already the person you want to be. Do whatever it takes. When babies learn to walk, they see everybody else around them walking, so they learn; they do whatever it takes. Every baby falls thousands of times learning, but what do they do? They laugh while falling forward.

I'm saying learn and have results rather than reasons why you didn't do it. Accept feedback. Make corrections, but get inside the act of your life as you want to be. If you want to have instant success, act as if you are a success now.

Be Coachable

Number eight: to have instant success, *be coachable*. I once went on a weeklong vacation of aikido skiing with Tom Crum, the master of trainers. Aikido is the highest form of martial arts. It is totally nonviolent. When somebody pushes on you, you just flow with them and use their own strength against themselves rather than against you. Aikido skiing means working with the flow of the energy lines in the mountain instead of against them. In one week, I went from being a green-level skier to black.

The first day, when I was with Tom, taking the chairlift up, he was talking about some of his other students. He trained Michael Jordan. Michael Jordan started out skiing, and he had fifty paparazzi around him. Every time he fell, he was like a little kid. He just laughed and chortled and was full of glee. He knew he was going to learn, because he was with the coach of coaches, Tom Crum.

It didn't matter how many times Michael fell or how many times the paparazzi took pictures of him falling. He knew that he was going to master skiing and go from green to black to a black mogul to a black double diamond skier, all in a week. Did he do it? Of course. Why? Because he was coachable when it was time to be coachable. He said, "Boss, what do I need to do here to improve?" He absorbed the information and executed it with elegance, verve, vitality, and savoir-faire.

You decide that you're going to be coachable. When I started my speaking business, I was upside down, I was broke, I was eating peanut butter until my tongue stuck to the roof of my mouth. But I asked everybody, "How do you find somebody that could coach me in the speaking business? Who else is young?" because until then everybody that was speaking had a cotton-top. They were medical doctors, lawyers, or celebrities. I was just a twenty-six-year-old kid without much experience (although I knew how to sell), and I needed to learn.

My roommate said, "There's a guy who trains in real estate. His name is Chip Collins." Within a half-hour of hearing that, I was in this guy's audience for the next three hours. He was also twenty-six, and he was wowing the audience. At that time (almost fifty years ago), he getting paid over $50,000 a year, and that sounded wonderful to my mind. I sat down with Chip and I said, "Look, I need you to mentor me through this." Because he saw that I had the burning desire in my eyes, he said, "I'll be your coach," and we met every week. He coached me through things that you can't even start to believe.

For example, one week I hadn't hit my sales quota, and if I didn't hit my sales quota, I wasn't going to make money. It was on a Friday night. We usually met at a diner in the middle of Long Island around 5:30, and we'd finish around 7:30. Chip said, "OK. Now I want you to go out and sell until you hit your goals."

"Nobody's available on a Friday night," I said.

"All the big guys are still working," he replied. "You've memorized where all those offices are. You just go to the office, and you'll see there's one car left. It's always the general agent or manager."

I went in to the managers; every time they were working, and there were no gatekeepers. I'd go in, and they said, "If you can teach our men and women how to sell like this, you've got the job." I got hired every time, and I always hit my quota. Sometimes it was at 11:30 or midnight on a Friday night, but it was astounding to me, because I was willing to be coachable by somebody that would coach me. The first three years in the businesses, I did a thousand talks a year. Later I met Tony Robbins and found that the two of us are probably the only crazy workaholics who put in that much energy to launch our respective careers. To get massive results, you must put in, and keep putting in, massive right action in the right direction. I loved it. I had a white-hot desire. I was eager and excited to become one of the best speakers ever.

If you don't have a coach, get a coach. Michael Jordan said, "I must have Phil Jackson coaching, or I can't continue to grow, play, and keep improving." If the best basketball player needs a coach in his field, so do you. We all need to be coached by somebody to get to instant success.

Network

The next point is to *network your way to instant success*. Your network will become your net worth if you're wise and judicious in whom you choose to put into it. By *network*, I mean the people you know, the people you get referrals from, contacts from, support from, and advice from. My teacher Cavett Robert, the dean of speakers in America, says, "You've got to make contacts to get contracts. You've got to have exposure to the max if you want to get success to the max."

Not only that, but you've got to get the right exposure to the right people, and this takes some thinking. It takes some reading. It takes a look at the newspaper, at some of the autobiographies and biographies of people in our time, so you can see whom you need to put your radar out for. You can align yourself with the who's who of, first, your area, then of your state, then maybe of the country. You could look at a book like the one about Dr. Armand Hammer. It's a picture book that gives you look at a week in Hammer's life. He dealt with the who's who of the world and traveled vast amounts.

You ask, "Why should I get to know the right people?" Because instant success has something to do with your future earning power. Your future earning power is hidden in what you know and whom you know who can get you to the people you need to know. Every one of us has a circle of influence of about two hundred and fifty people. Look at the average wedding or funeral; the attendance is about two hundred and fifty.

You may say, "I can't get to that many people fast." Let me give you my own little experience. My daddy died unexpectedly, at least to me. I thought he was going to live to be 107, because I had an uncle that old. My little brother, who's an attorney, had written his will. My dad called me up in advance and said, "Boy, I'm going home one last time." I wasn't listening at the right level, so I bypassed what my dad was really saying. He was coming home from hospice. I would have wanted to travel home and hold his hand on his way out, but Dad went home and died in the bed that he was born in back in Denmark.

My little brother called me up on July 4 and said, "Dad died." My little brother's a great humorist, and I thought he was giving me some black humor, so I didn't get it. He said, "No, I'm serious. Dad died. He wrote in the funeral that you're to call all of his 258 cronies to come to the funeral. You've got two days to pull it off, big brother."

I was in absolute shock, but because it was my dad's final wish, I called every one of them in the next two days, and most of them came to my dad's funeral.

The point is, every one of us has a list of people we can get to. You need to look over that list. If you don't have whom you want on it, write down in your imagination whom you'd like to have on it.

As a matter of fact, why not write a contact list of the next two hundred and fifty people you'd like to befriend over time? Your life can start with one little contact, and you can go anywhere you want to go.

When Chip Collins advised me on how to build a speaking business, he said, "I'm in the real estate business, so you've got to stay out of that. I'll let you have the life insurance business. It's a bottomless pit for motivation. You'll never run out."

"But look," I said. "I don't own any life insurance. All I've got after going bankrupt is one suit. I've got this beat-up old Volkswagen. I'm a little bit afraid. I don't know what CLU means." I didn't know it meant *chartered life underwriter*. (The joke, of course, is that it stands for "cunning, lonely, and unhappy.") Chip said, "You'll call on ten offices, you'll meet one guy, and you'll be home." I believed him. I called on the last person, the tenth person.

It's 4:30 p.m. in the Metropolitan Life Insurance office on Long Island. A big guy, a lovely Italian gentleman as big as Pavarotti, takes me in. Not only does he hire me, but he says, "Here, boy. Here's a directory. You call everybody and tell them Tony called you."

That's what I mean. You can get to anyone from one person, if you know that one person. The cliché says we are never more than six people away from the person that we want to meet.

It doesn't matter who the person is, or the situation or circumstance. Ask yourself, how can this person help me achieve my goal? Back when Jack and I were starting to sell Chicken Soup titles, I said, "What can we learn that could be helpful for us to sell more Chicken Soups?" We kept asking ourselves that question. We lived in the question. When you live in the question—how am I going to network? How am I going to meet the right people to get the right results right here and right now?—you'll do it.

My friend Harvey Mackay, who wrote *Swim with Sharks without Getting Eaten Alive*, says, "Whoever has the biggest Rolodex wins in the future," because your network is your net worth. He has a list of about six thousand contact that just keeps growing and glowing. At one point he said, "My daughter's going through high school. I think every high school kid should be ashamed to graduate unless they've got five hundred contacts."

So Harvey had a business card made for his daughter. She started giving it out and asking for other people's business cards. By the time she graduated high school, she had five hundred contacts. She got a job in Germany for the summer. She was paid three times more than anyone else in her class. She learned the language fluently and got to travel to Europe the whole summer.

When my daughters were little, both of them were in Girl Scouts. I believe that every girl should be in Girl Scouts and every boy in Boy Scouts or the equivalent, because that's a way to grow up to be an instant success.

I got my daughters little business cards. I gave them out to all our friends. Like they'd give one to someone and say, "My name's Elizabeth Day Hansen, and here's my business card. I'd like to earn the right to do business with you."

Sure enough, the adults that I hang out with all said yes. When it was time to sell Girl Scout cookies, she called 134 people and sold more than anyone in Southern California with a little telemarketing script that I gave her.

It's easy to build a network for a little kid. It's also easy for a big kid—you. Why not check out what the ten top businesspeople you know did to build their network? Then do what they did.

There's an idea in *The Celestine Prophecy*, by James Redfield: if your attitude's open and right, the next person you need will have the solution to your problem or the next opportunity for your instant success.

Expand and Contract Time

My final concept for instant success is *expand and contract time*. Let me give you an example.

Sylvester "Sly" Stallone once watched a movie about Muhammad Ali on TV. At that time, Sly was a B-grade movie actor.

Up until then, Sly had no visible means of success, but on the screen of his imagination, once he watched Muhammad Ali, he said, "I can write a movie that will be a brilliant screenplay and has honor, dignity, courage, savoir-faire, and panache." He locked himself in a room for three days and three nights, wrote the script of *Rocky*, and went to Hollywood to sell it. The studio gave him a check for $375,000.

Sly said, "I want the lead role."

They said, "No way. Get out of here."

Sly somehow had the courage to rip up the check and give it back. He went out and raised $1 million to make the picture. The rest is history. *Rocky* did sequels, and Sly went on to get advances of $20 million to write, produce, and star in feature films. He took ownership of his time and his life to command and demand a future worthy of his vision.

Here's my question to you: what is your vision of the future? Because if your vision's big enough and you need to, you can literally contract time or expand it, because time is plastic. It's malleable. It's changeable. It'll do anything you want with it. You can get more out of less time if you know what you want in your heart of hearts. As a student of time control and wanting to master everlasting results, I've monitored the president of the United States. He is essentially in charge of the free world, and as such, he has a lot to think about in order to make a difference and leave a legacy before he gets out of office. Daily he goes into the White House, and the world's on fire, metaphorically speaking. He has to decide what needs to be done and to delegate it decisively and correctly.

Some parts of the president's job description also belong to you and me. Each president has a chief of staff whose job it is to be comprehensively wise and see to it that the boss gets to look at issues that matter and meets with the right leaders at the right time in the right way to get the right results right here and right now, along with the necessary photo ops and even a little restful pleasure on the side.

If you don't have a person who's going to leverage you and multiply your effectiveness, you need to write down as one of your goals to have one. Each of us needs force multipliers. That person can instantly double your earnings if you'll let him or her. You need to have a support person so you can do what my friend Dan Sullivan says: "Delegate everything but your genius. Genius is that rare talent that you express and deliver brilliantly." As the cliché goes, Frank Sinatra did not move pianos.

The president of the United States does something I'm going to ask you to do. He gets three files a day. He gets a red file early in the morning, during breakfast. The president's red file contains his schedule for the day and the decisions he must make. It demands his urgent attention and frequently causes him to reschedule his day.

As a bonus point here, my friend Ken Blanchard says, "Get the time management monkey off your back. Have your subordinate write out three possible solutions, and highlight the best one before you even look at them."

Let me give you proof of this. Once I sat in an airplane with one of Ronald Reagan's first lieutenants. He unfortunately had to break the news to the president about the savings and loans crisis, which looked as if it would cost $680 billion and bankrupt America. When Reagan got the news, it didn't faze him in the least. He looked right back at his lieutenant and said, "And what are you going to do about it?" That's magnificence in time leadership. A man eventually came with three solutions, chose the most effective one, and proceeded to solve the problem. Subpoint: if leaders absorb their problems and become immobilized by them, as Jimmy Carter did with the Iran hostage crisis, they're useless.

File number two for the president is a green file, full of important, must-do tasks. File number three contains information, letters, ideas, and calls to get to as he can.

Once during the Clinton administration, I was staying at the penthouse of the Sheraton Hotel by the White House. I'd gotten back after a hard day's work. The street in front of the hotel was barricaded and jammed with police to escort President Clinton from the hotel.

Watching the procession of limos and Secret Service agents as it formed, I had a bird's-eye view of the president as he was handed his three files to review at 11:00 p.m. en route back to the White House. It astounded me to witness his full energy at the end of a busy day, with an official dinner, and yet he had to read correspondence, political positions, and global reports on the way home.

I was inspired, because I'd used the same folder system, which I'd read about years ago. Now if the president uses that to have instant time control, even if you don't have an assistant, employ it now, and deploy it on your assistant, so later on you can have even more instant success.

At this point I'm going to carry you from where you are to where you want to be. Right now, visualize your heart's desire. I don't care what it is—a new home, a business that's flourishing, a life and a lifestyle that are opulent and energetic, such that you can entertain the who's who of the world. They're coming up into your estate, which is speckled by beautiful, blooming flowers. It smells wonderful, and you're the king or queen of the hill.

That's what I'm going to give you now: instant success, so you can reach the ultimate in your life and have all the good that you could imagine and desire, and have fun doing it.

In concluding, let me share a poem by my friend, author Marianne Williamson. It's called "Our Deepest Fear":

Our deepest fear is not that we are inadequate.
Our deepest fear is that we are powerful beyond measure.
It is our light, not our darkness
That most frightens us.

We ask ourselves
Who am I to be brilliant, gorgeous, talented, fabulous?
Actually, who are you not to be?
You are a child of God.

Your playing small
Does not serve the world.
There's nothing enlightened about shrinking
So that other people won't feel insecure around you.

We are all meant to shine,
As children do.
We were born to make manifest
The glory of God that is within us.

It's not just in some of us;
It's in everyone.

And as we let our own light shine,
We unconsciously give other people permission to do the same.
As we're liberated from our own fear,
Our presence automatically liberates others.